PALLADIUS:
THE LAUSIAC HISTORY

Ancient Christian Writers

THE WORKS OF THE FATHERS IN TRANSLATION

EDITED BY

JOHANNES QUASTEN   WALTER J. BURGHARDT,

THOMAS COMERFORD LAWLER

No. 34

WESTMINSTER, MARYLAND

THE NEWMAN PRESS

LONDON

LONGMANS, GREEN AND CO.

1965

PALLADIUS:

THE LAUSIAC HISTORY

TRANSLATED AND ANNOTATED

BY

ROBERT T. MEYER, Ph.D.

Professor of Classical Philology
Catholic University of America
Washington, D.C.

WESTMINSTER, MARYLAND
THE NEWMAN PRESS

LONDON
LONGMANS, GREEN AND CO.
1965

THE NEWMAN PRESS
WESTMINSTER, MD., U.S.A.

LONGMANS, GREEN AND CO LTD
48 GROSVENOR STREET, LONDON W 1

RAILWAY CRESCENT, CROYDON, VICTORIA, AUSTRALIA
AUCKLAND, KINGSTON (JAMAICA), LAHORE, NAIROBI

LONGMANS SOUTHERN AFRICA (PTY) LTD
THIBAULT HOUSE, THIBAULT SQUARE, CAPE TOWN
JOHANNESBURG, SALISBURY

LONGMANS OF NIGERIA LTD
W. R. INDUSTRIAL ESTATE, IKEJA

LONGMANS OF GHANA LTD
INDUSTRIAL ESTATE, RING ROAD SOUTH, ACCRA

LONGMANS GREEN (FAR EAST) LTD
443 LOCKHART ROAD, HONG KONG

LONGMANS OF MALAYSIA LTD
44 JALAN AMPANG, KUALA LUMPUR

ORIENT LONGMANS LTD
CALCUTTA, BOMBAY, MADRAS
DELHI, HYDERABAD, DACCA

LONGMANS CANADA LTD
137 BOND STREET, TORONTO 2

First published in U.S.A. 1965
First published in Great Britain 1965

LIBRARY OF CONGRESS CATALOG CARD NUMBER: 65-18184

De Licentia Superioris S.J.
Nihil obstat: J. QUASTEN, cens. dep.
Imprimatur: PATRICIUS A. O'BOYLE, D.D., Archiep. Washingtonen.
d. 22 Maii 1964

MADE AND PRINTED IN USA
BY YORK COMPOSITION CO., INC., YORK, PA.

CONTENTS

v

PALLADIUS:
THE LAUSIAC HISTORY

INTRODUCTION

"There are in Egypt men who, desirous of living a life like that of angels, have sequestered themselves from the tumult of cities to dwell in deserts, and who among these barren sands produce by their extraordinary virtues fruit pleasing to God. . . ."

—THEODORET[1]

The two most important source documents for the history of early monasticism in Egypt, where monasticism had its beginnings, are the celebrated *Life of Saint Antony* by the great Saint Athanasius and the *Lausiac History* by Palladius. The first of these, written about the year 357 A.D., has already appeared in the present series.[2] The second, composed about sixty years after Athanasius' book, is now offered here in new English translation. The title of the book derives from the name of the person to whom it was dedicated.

The historical value of both these works lies largely in the fact that the author of each had for a time himself lived the monastic life in the desert and knew at first hand whereof he spoke. Also, each writer complements the other. The first, in Saint Antony's "Address to the Monks,"[3] gives a long treatise on the theoretical aspect of the ascetic life. Palladius restricts himself almost entirely

3

to straightforward accounts of what he had personally seen or experienced and of what he had received in the way of similar stories from others. The biography of Antony is centered in Egypt. The *Lausiac History* describes monastic life not only in Egypt but in Palestine, Syria, and Asia Minor as well.

The purpose in each case was to edify. Athanasius addressed his *Vita Antonii* "to the brethren in foreign parts," *ad peregrinos fratres,* to men who were living the religious life and attempting to rival even the Egyptian monks in their austerity;[4] "and I feel that you also," he wrote, "once you have heard the story, will not merely admire the man but will wish to emulate his resolution as well."[5] Palladius, who took time out from a busy life to write biographic sketches or notes on some sixty holy men and women he had met or heard about, dedicated his work to Lausus, the royal chamberlain at the court of Emperor Theodosius II. This was at a time when the Church, newly liberated from the catacombs, was in a period of *lithomania,*[6] a madness as it were for great ecclesiastical edifices. Palladius wished to teach Lausus lessons of true edification, the building and formation of character modeled on the lives of the desert saints. Among his stories of holy men and women Palladius includes accounts of individuals who fell from virtue because of excessive pride, some of them returning to grace once again through God's holy grace. Palladius thus shows that sackcloth alone does not make the monk, and he tells us that he felt constrained to record such incidents so that we might know the danger of pride and the power of prayer.

PALLADIUS' LIFE AND WORKS

Aside from some few remarks by contemporaries, our knowledge of Palladius' life comes only from the sifting of details from two of his writings, the *Historia Lausiaca* and the *Dialogus de vita sancti Joannis Chrysostomi.*[7] He was born in 363 or 364 in Galatia. A pupil of the famed Evagrius of Pontus, he received a thorough education in the classics. Of his immediate family we know virtually nothing. A reference in the *Historia Lausiaca* lets us know that in 394 his father was still alive and that his brother and sister had embraced the religious life.[8] From the *Dialogus* we learn that the brother, named Brisson, had earlier left the Church of his own free will and had been living on a small farm, working his land himself.[9]

When he was twenty-three years old, Palladius embraced the monastic life as a disciple of Innocent on the Mount of Olives.[10] He stayed for a while with a certain Elpidius near Jericho, and then in or about the year 388 he set out to become acquainted with the Egyptian hermits.[11] He spent a total of about three years in Alexandria and in the so-called Solitudes not far from that city. Then he went on to Nitria, and subsequently proceeded from there to Cellia, where he stayed for nine years. His health broke down and he returned to Alexandria for medical treatment. When the physicians in Alexandria advised a change of climate, he left Egypt for the "better air" of Palestine. The following year, 400, he went to Bithynia where he was consecrated bishop of Helenopolis, probably by Saint John Chrysostom. He was appointed to a commission set up to investigate charges made against Antoninus, bishop of Ephesus, by Eusebius, the bishop of

Valentinopolis.[12] He spent the summer and autumn in Asia Minor before returning to his own see of Helenopolis.

In the year 403 he appeared along with Saint John Chrysostom at the famous Synod of the Oak which had been called near Chalcedon by Chrysostom's enemy, Theophilus of Alexandria. Chrysostom was there condemned on a number of fabricated counts and deposed from his position as patriarch of Constantinople, and Palladius himself was questioned as to his own Origenism. After a stormy time in John Chrysostom's company in Constantinople, Palladius fled the civil authorities and in 405 journeyed to Rome to plead Chrysostom's cause before Pope Innocent I. When he returned to Constantinople, he was arrested together with a group of companions and eventually was exiled by the Emperor Arcadius to Egypt. It was while living there in exile at Syene in the years 406–408 that he wrote the *Dialogus*. After Syene he spent four years at Antinoë in the Thebaid.[13]

When the opposition to John Chrysostom finally came to an end in 412, Palladius went back to Galatia. There, as he tells us in the *Historia Lausiaca*,[14] he knew a priest named Philoromus, and he may have lived for a time with him. The church historian Socrates lists Palladius as having been transferred from the see of Helenopolis to that of Aspuna.[15] Of Palladius' death we know nothing of either the time or the circumstances. Evidently he was already dead in 431, as we know that another bishop from his see attended the Council of Ephesus that year.

If we can accept Palladian authorship of the *Epistola de Indicis gentibus et de Bragmanibus*,[16] a work which has survived under the name of Palladius but which may in whole or in part have been written by others, our author made a trip to the borders of India in the company of a bishop Moses of Adoule. It is possible that Palladius did in fact make such a journey, although we do not know exactly when this would have been. Since the *Historia Lausiaca*, a wide-ranging work, does not mention it, we are probably safe in assuming that any such trip, if made, was in the latter part of his life.

HISTORICAL RELIABILITY

The *Lausiac History*, written about 419 or 420, is, of course, the work by which Palladius is best known. Palladius had traveled much and listened much, and he might deservingly be called the Herodotus of the Desert Fathers. His *History* is peopled with numerous personages who also appear in the anonymous *Historia monachorum in Aegypto*[17] and in the various collections of unknown authorship called the *Apophthegmata patrum* or *Verba seniorum*.[18] Some of the people he writes about are well known—Jerome of Stridon, Athanasius, Pachomius, Evagrius of Pontus, and others—while some are known not at all beyond the mention of them by Palladius. At least one of our writer's sources was literary, for he specifically mentions Saint Athanasius' *Life of Saint Antony*.[19] As might be expected, Palladius' work is permeated with the spirit of his great teacher, the founder of monastic mysticism, Evagrius of Pontus.[20]

Although the importance of the *Lausiac History* for the history of early monasticism had long been recognized, in the nineteenth century the veracity of Palladius was for a time questioned[21]—but was just as vigorously upheld.[22] The distinguished Coptic scholar E. Amélineau approached the whole reliability question from the base of the Christian archaeology of Egypt. Amélineau vouches for the accuracy of Palladius and is convinced that our writer actually visited the places mentioned in his *History*. [23] Amélineau warns, however, that caution is necessary where Palladius depended upon hearsay. Today the *Lausiac History* is accepted as a true account, but with due recognition given the fact that there are some passages marked by hyperbole and that Palladius accepted some stories from others (including possibly in some cases stories in written form) which are dubious.[24]

It should also be noted here that the three introductory pieces which precede the *History* proper—the Foreword, the Letter to Lausus, and the Prologue—are not written in the same style of Greek as is the main body of the work. These three items are written in a more literary and more stilted style. The Foreword, moreover, does not appear in the manuscripts of the best tradition, and of the three parts in question here it is the least likely to be genuinely Palladian. There is less reason to question the texts we have of the Letter to Lausus and the Prologue. In fact in all three cases it may well be that the noted differences in style stem from nothing more than efforts by Palladius to put the final touches to his work in the best—and most flowery—language of which he was capable.

THE TEXTUAL PROBLEM

The history of the Greek text as composed by Palladius was for a long time a puzzle and indeed some aspects of the textual problem are by no means entirely settled even to-day. The popularity that the *Lausiac History* enjoyed re-sulted in its being copied and reworked many times and it was widely used for both devotional and entertainment purposes. Dom Cuthbert Butler, whose magnificent work in the field replaced textual confusion with order, wrote of Palladius' *History:*

> "So popular was it that no respect whatever was felt for its text: it was re-written, re-arranged, enlarged, short-ened, paraphrased, combined with kindred works, with-out any scruple. Thus every known process of corruption—revision, interpolation, redaction, inter-mixture of texts—has had free play among the MSS. both of the Greek texts and the versions."[25]

From very early times there existed two Greek recensions, a long and a short redaction, entirely contradictory in parts. The picture was further complicated by the exist-ence of many versions in Latin, into which tongue the *History* had been translated at an early date. Oriental translations from the Greek had also been made in number.

Syriac. In the Syriac, for example, there are two in-dependent versions of equal antiquity.[26] Anan-Isho, a Nes-torian monk in Mesopotamia in the seventh century, collected together the then-current Syriac *apophthegmata* of the leading Egyptian monks. These he included in a large work he called the "Paradise of the Fathers," in-corporating therein "the histories of the Holy Fathers composed by Palladius and Jerome."[27] We must think of his work as a *bibliotheca*, "library," of ascetic writings rather than a single work, as it also contained a Syriac version of Saint Athanasius' *Life of Saint Antony.*[28] An-other Syriac version represented in various manuscripts in the Vatican Library and the British Museum may be as old as the version by Anan-Isho. Moreover, many Syriac collections of *apophthegmata* contain extracts from Palladius, and even the so-called "Laughable Stories" of Bar-Hebraeus includes three episodes from Palladius.[29]

Armenian. The Armenian version[30] appears to be a paraphrase rather than a strict translation. It is possible that it was made from the Syriac rather than directly from the Greek of Palladius. In the nineteenth century the Mechitarian Fathers of St. Lazzaro printed two volumes of Armenian *Lives of the Holy Fathers* (Venice 1855); the lives of Paul the Simple and Macarius of Alexandria included in this collection appear to be free paraphrases of Palladian material. There is in the Armenian a certain amount of confusion in the handling of subject matter; in some places, for example, two separate incidents of a saint's life are blended into one. Butler has shown how there apparently was at times a misunderstanding of the Greek original.[31]

Coptic. Butler devoted almost fifty pages to a discussion of the Coptic version.[32] Some of the extant Coptic fragments, notably the introductory letter to Lausus, are certainly translations from the Greek. Some statements in the Coptic which are not found elsewhere can be explained as the result of misunderstandings of the original Greek text. In other places, where the Coptic version actually does contain matter not in the Palladian account, Butler found that the inserted material had been taken from other Greek works such as, for example, the *Ecclesiastical History* of Socrates.

Ethiopic. An Ethiopic version exists in fragments[33] as the first of the three "Rules of Pachomius" printed in

Dillmann's *Chrestomathia Aethiopica* (Berlin 1866). Wherever readings in this version appear to differ from those in the Greek text, support for the Ethiopic readings can be found in one or the other of extant Greek manuscripts. It is quite possible, as Butler pointed out, that an examination of such works as "Histories of Our Holy Fathers" or "Garden of the Monks" mentioned in the manuscript catalogues of the Ethiopic collections of the Vatican, the British Museum, or the Bodleian Libraries may prove to go back to the time of Palladius.

Arabic. As for Arabic versions[34] we have first of all an Arabic translation of the Syriac "Paradise of the Fathers" mentioned above. There is also a *Vita Pachomii* which was translated into Arabic from the Coptic. Some manuscript catalogues also list books in Arabic whose titles lead us to believe they might contain genuine Palladian material.

Old Sogdian. Quite recently we have learned of yet another Oriental version, a fragment from the Old Sogdian.[35] This version actually stems from the long recension of the Palladius text and therefore, as will be seen below, is not truly Palladian. The existence of this version does serve, however, to show the spread of these accounts of the Egyptian monks to Central Asia at an early period.

MODERN STUDIES, CRITICISM, AND EDITIONS

The number of the various versions referred to above is testimony to the extreme popularity of the *Lausiac History* in the East as well as in the West. The textual picture, however, which had been confused for centuries, was clarified only around the turn of the last century through

the work of the Benedictine scholar Dom Cuthbert Butler.[36]

Butler proved quite conclusively that of the two Greek
recensions, the longer, which he called B, was the metaphrastic text, an enlarged and greatly ornamented redaction of a briefer text, which Butler called G. The so-called
G text, the shorter and simpler form, is found in only a
very small number of known Greek manuscripts. It is,
however, the basis of the principal early versions, two
Latin and the two early Syriac translations mentioned
above. Butler was the first to print the G text. His work
was promptly hailed as a monument to scholarship and
learning, as great a crown to modern Benedictine industry
as the best work of the Benedictines in the eighteenth century.[37] Although critics were not slow to come forward to
attack the Butler text on fine points,[38] no one to this day
has offered a completely satisfactory replacement.

When Butler in 1921 replied[39] to the criticisms, he said
that he agreed that he had relied too strongly on the Paris
manuscript (P) and should have paid more attention to an
Oxford manuscript which he had found too late to in-
corporate in his edition except for the addition of some of
the most significant readings from it. He noted, however,
that P was still the principal manuscript, as it contains the
complete *History*, while other manuscripts of the G group
contain only fragments. He stated (and we must take these
words as his final judgment on his own work): "Were I
to undertake now to re-edit the text, I would give less
weight to P and greater weight to the variants (strictly so
called) of T [a manuscript of Turin which Butler had
used for his critical edition but which was lost in a fire in
1903] certainly when supported by another witness to

the text."[40] But, he added, while the text would thus be improved in many places, it would not be substantially altered.

Nothing more of a critical study appeared until 1938. E. Schwartz, who had been using photographs of the Oxford manuscript Wake 67 to study Cyril of Scythopolis' *Life of Euthymius,* had found inserted therein a misplaced folio which contained the conclusion of Palladius' *Lausiac History.* Schwartz collated this page with the text of Dom Butler and published the variants.[41]

The next to take up the cudgels was Mgr. René Draguet of Louvain. He had begun a translation of Palladius for the French series *Sources chrétiennes* as early as 1942,[42] planning a full historical commentary. He had faithfully followed the text published by Butler and had planned to reprint this text with his translation. The text was photographed and announced as in the press in December 1946. Mgr. Draguet, however, then first saw the article of Schwartz which had been published in 1938 but which had come to Draguet only after World War II was over. Draguet had been busy with the source problem of Palladius and he now reported that his faith in the Butler edition was somewhat shaken.[43] Not long thereafter Draguet had occasion to consult a manuscript at Athens which threw new light on the G group, and he published his findings in 1949.[44] The manuscript in question here was one which had been known to Butler, although Butler had not actually seen it. Draguet himself admitted that even if Butler had been able to use this particular manuscript, it would not have been of much help, as it simply confirms what he had already known of manuscripts of the G group. Then in 1950 Draguet published an article[45] in which he claimed that Butler had not paid enough attention to the Wake 67 manuscript of Christ Church, Oxford. A defense of Butler against Draguet was published in 1955 by D. J. Chitty.[46] This in turn provoked a rejoinder the same year from the Louvain savant beginning with a trenchant statement that Butler's "case" is a bad one and Chitty was indeed an "ill-favored advocate."[47]

Since that time there has been nothing more published on the subject of Palladius from the pen of Mgr. Draguet. He has, however, kindly addressed a letter to the present translator in which he remarks that everyone will understand why the Butler text must form the basis for the present translation. Until better Greek manuscripts of the G type are found, Dom Butler's text must be considered the best text available and the basis for any new work on the *Lausiac History* that will be done in the future.[48]

The first edition of the Greek text of the *History* to appear after Butler's work was that prepared by A. Lucot and published by him with a French translation in 1912.[49] Lucot followed the Butler text but added some different readings which had been suggested by the critics of Butler. Lucot broke the text down into numbered paragraphs; his numbering has since been accepted as standard. He also shows himself more of a *philologue* than Butler; I found some of his notes on the late Greek vocabulary of Palladius very useful and his translation as well proved helpful in places.

In 1927 there appeared the edition of Dom Antoni Ramon,[50] a Benedictine monk from the Abbey of Montserrat who was able while teaching in Jerusalem to utilize certain Greek manuscripts of Palladius which had not been

known to Butler or which had been known to him only
through entries in manuscript catalogues. Nevertheless
Ramon tells us[51] that his text is fundamentally that of
Butler. Ramon followed the paragraph numbering of Lucot and published a selected list of textual variants. This
Bernat Series edition of the text includes a translation of
the *History* into Catalan.

In preparing the present translation I have followed the
Butler text except in a few places (each of these is pointed
out in the Notes) where I have followed different readings as given by Lucot. The paragraph numbering I have
used is that which was established by Lucot. The earlier
English translation published in 1918 by W. K. L. Clarke[52]
I found a great help at times. There is also a German translation by S. Krottenthaler,[53] published in 1912, which was
of some service. The Slavic translation by Partenij[54] was
not available to me. Selections from Palladius are given in
Danish translation in a work published in 1955 by H. F.
Johannsen.[55]

It remains for me to thank the Rev. Edgar R. Smothers,
S.J., of the Bellarmine School of Theology, North Aurora,
Illinois, for having so kindly read my translation in its
early stages and for making many valuable suggestions.

FOREWORD

TO THE LIFE OF THE HOLY FATHERS[1]

1. In this book is recorded the wonderfully virtuous and ascetic life of the holy fathers, monks, and anchorites of the desert. It is written for the emulation[2] and imitation of those who wish to succeed in the heavenly way of life and to take the journey which leads to the kingdom of heaven. It is written also to commemorate women far advanced in years and illustrious God-inspired mothers who have performed feats of virtuous asceticism in strong and perfect intention,[3] as exemplars and models for those women who wish to wear the crown of self-abnegation and chastity.

2. It was written at the suggestion of one of the finest of men, one who was most learned in my opinion, of peaceable habits, religiously disposed in heart and mind, and charitable to the poor. It was this man, highly honored as he was, and by reason of his own goodness occupying a high place among great men, guided by the power of the Spirit of God—he it was who enjoined us to this task. Or, rather, it was he who aroused our sluggish mind to the contemplation of higher things. Indeed, it was he who moved us to imitate and rival the ascetic virtues of the holy and immortal spiritual fathers, those who had led lives pleasing to God by subjecting their own bodies.

3. Now that we have written the lives of these uncon-

quered athletes,[4] thereby publishing the outstanding virtues of each and every one of these great and holy men, we dedicate the work to him. This is none other than Lausus,[5] the best of men, who loves this pious and spiritual zeal. Through the influence of God he has been appointed guardian of our holy and revered empire.

4. Untutored as I am in the use of language,[6] and having but slight knowledge of the spiritual, I myself felt unequal to the task of cataloguing the holy fathers in the spiritual life. I feared the magnitude of the undertaking. Then, too, I was greatly perturbed at the command which calls for knowledge of worldly as well as spiritual wisdom. But in the first place I have great respect for the earnest virtue of the man who spurred us on to this task. Secondly I thought of the help this account would be to those who read it. Moreover, I was afraid of the danger that lies in the plausible excuse. Therefore, referring the noble undertaking to Providence, I fell to with great earnestness. I went to the contests in the arena, provided with the wings of the holy fathers' intercession. I leave you an account now, an epitome as it were, of merely the outstanding ascetic practices and miracles of the noble athletes and great men —and not only of men famous for their strict way of life, but of holy highborn women, too, who lived the best and loftiest lives.

5. And I was deemed worthy to see for myself the revered and devout countenances of those who had already perfected themselves in the arena of piety.[7] I learned of their heavenly way of life from inspired athletes of Christ. I traveled on foot and looked into every cave and cabin of the monks of the desert with all accuracy and pious motive. I wrote down some of the things I saw, and also

some accounts I heard from the holy fathers. It is all in this book—the contests of the great men, and of the women, too, more like men in their nature than the name implies, thanks to their hope in Christ. I send it to you so that you might hear the account of these godly people, for you are the ornament of the best of those who love God as well as the honor of the most faithful and divinely favored empire. Noble and Christ-beloved servant of God, Lausus, I have recorded to the utmost of my poor ability the glorious name of each of the athletes of Christ, men and women alike. I have recorded only a few of their lesser contests, and in most cases I have added the family, the town, and the place of the monastery.

6. We have commemorated men and women who aimed at the highest virtue, but who in many cases were pulled down toward the deep pit of hell by vainglory, the so-called mother of pride. The perfection of asceticism which they had desired, and for which they had struggled and worked hard for so long a time, was lost in one minute by pride and self-esteem. But they were snatched from the snares of the devil by the grace of our Saviour, the vigilance of the holy fathers, the sympathetic compassion of spiritual friends, and so were restored to their former virtuous life by the prayers of the saints.[8]

LETTER TO LAUSUS THE ROYAL CHAMBERLAIN WRITTEN BY PALLADIUS THE BISHOP[9]

1. I wish you success in your resolution—for it is only right that I begin the letter with an expression of good wishes. While others are all imitating vain things and building with stones which will not make them happy, you desire to be taught the words of true edification.[10] For the God of all is alone untaught, since He is self-existent and was preceded by no other being; all others are taught, since they are made and created. The first order of beings have their learning from the most high Trinity, the second learns from the first, the third from the second, and so on down to the least. Those who are higher in knowledge and virtue teach the lower.[11]

2. Now those who think they need no teacher, or those who do not believe those who teach them in the way of love, are afflicted with the disease of ignorance, which is the mother of overweening pride. They are preceded in the way of destruction by those who have fallen from the heavenly path, the demons who fly about in the air, having left their heavenly teachers. For words and syllables do not constitute teaching—sometimes those who possess these are disreputable in the extreme—but teaching consists of virtuous acts of conduct, of freedom from injuriousness, of dauntlessness, and of an even temper. To all these add an intrepidity which produces words like flames of fire.

3. For if this were not so, the great Teacher would not have told His disciples: *Learn of me, because I am meek and humble of heart.*[12] He did not use fine language when teaching them, but He required rather the formation of their character, causing grief only to those who hate the Word and teachers as well. For the soul being trained to act in accord with God's plan must either learn faithfully what it does not know, or teach clearly what it does know. But if it is unwilling to do either, even though it is able, then it suffers madness. For this is the beginning of apostasy, to be full of learning and yet not desire the Word for which the soul of a lover of God hungers.[13] Take courage, be strong, and be a man! May God grant that you follow in the knowledge of Christ.

PROLOGUE

1. Numerous writers have bequeathed to their times various writings of different types about different things.[14] Some have written with the inspiration of the grace given by God above for the edification and safety of those who follow the teachings of the Saviour with trusting intention. Others have gone to excess in their desire to please men and have written with corrupt purpose to reassure those who crave empty fame. Still others were inspired by a certain madness; intent upon the destruction of fickle men, with the energy of the demon who hates all good and in blind temper they have attacked the spotless purity of the Catholic Church by turning the minds of the foolish to hatred of the saintly way of life.

2. I, your humble servant, decided to honor Your Majesty's command, which was directed to your spiritual progress. I decided then, O man most fond of learning, to set forth for you an account of my entire experience. It was the thirty-third year of my being in the company of the brethren and of my own solitary life, my twentieth year as bishop, and the fifty-sixth year of my life as a whole. Now you wanted stories of the fathers, of both male and female anchorites, those I had seen and others I had heard about, and of those I had lived with in the Egyptian desert and Libya, in the Thebaid and Syene. Then there are the Tabennesiotes,[15] and those in Meso-

potamia, Palestine, and Syria, and, in the West, those in Rome and Campania and points near by.

3. May this account, then, be a sacred reminder for the good of your soul and a constant medicine against forgetfulness. May it dispel the drowsiness which arises from senseless desire, indecision, and pettiness in necessary affairs. May it free your character of hesitation and meanness of spirit. May it rid you of excitability, disorders, worldly conceit, and irrational fear. May it improve your neverfailing desire and your pious intention, and may it be a guide both to you and to those who are with you, not only your subordinates but your rulers as well. All those who love Christ make haste to be joined to God through these virtuous acts, each day preparing for the release of the soul, as is written:

4. It is good *to be dissolved and to be with Christ.*[16] And again: *Prepare thy work without, and diligently till thy ground.*[17] For he who always thinks of death as something which cannot be avoided or delayed, cannot go far astray.[18] Neither will he be misled in regard to suggestions of guidance, nor will he spurn my crude and unpolished manner of speech. For indeed it is not the aim of God's teaching to speak in learned fashion, but rather to win the mind over to the knowledge of truth, as has been said: *Open thy mouth for the word of God;*[19] and again: *Despise not the discourse of them that are ancient and wise, but acquaint thyself with their proverbs.*[20]

5. Thus, O lover of divine learning, I followed this adage in part and met many of the saints. While I made no precise calculation, I would make a journey of thirty days, or twice that, and covered on foot, God help me, the whole land of the Romans,[21] and I accepted the hardship

of travel gladly in order to meet a man full of the love of God and to gain what I lacked.

6. For if Paul, so much my superior in way of life and in knowledge, in conscience and faith, made a journey from Tarsus to Judea to meet with Peter, James, and John —if he boasted of this, putting it on a pedestal, as it were, saying: *I went to Jerusalem to see Peter,*[22] it was in order to relate his own trials as an incentive to those who lived in self-satisfaction and idleness. He was not satisfied merely to hear of Peter's virtue, but he longed for a meeting with him. How much more is it so that I should not be owed ten thousand talents[23] for doing the same, not so much to do them a good turn as to help myself!

7. For even those who wrote down the lives of the Fathers, Abraham and those in succession, Moses, Elias, and John, wrote not to glorify them, but to help their readers. Being aware of this, therefore, O most trusted servant of Christ, Lausus, take a warning for yourself and bear up with my nonsense, which acts to safeguard your pious mind. Your mind is by its nature subject to various evil influences, both seen and unseen; it can be at rest only with the aid of continual prayer and concern for its own salvation.

8. For many of the brethren prided themselves on their labors and almsgiving and boasted of their celibacy or their virginity; they had every confidence in attention to divine prophecies and to acts of zeal, and still they never attained a state of quietude. Without making inquiry they leaped to false conclusions and are ill of restlessness of life. In your actions you give in to curiosity; this in turn leads to evil acts and sets back the good advancement which had already been achieved.

9. Act the man then, I pray you. Do not build up your wealth. You have in fact been following this precept, since you have been diminishing your wealth on your own initiative by distributing to the needy. This has been a virtuous service. You have not bound your free will with an oath on a sudden impulse and without full consideration simply in order to win the praise of men. Some have done so in a spirit of rivalry and out of love for glory. They enslaved their own free will by the bond of an oath not to eat or drink. Then they fell again, true objects of pity, into their old love of life and into a state of spiritual torpor and pleasure—and so added to the former the fresh insult of perjury. Now you will not commit sin if you eat in moderation and restrain yourself reasonably.

10. For among our emotions reason partakes of the divine as it expels the harmful and accepts the helpful. Because *the law is not made for the just man.*[24] Now drinking wine within reason is better by far than drinking water in arrogance. For my sake, please look at the holy men who drink wine within the bounds of reason, then look at the corrupt men who drink water without moderation. Do not blame or praise the material itself, but deem blessed or unhappy the intention of those who use the material well or badly. Joseph at one time drank wine in Egypt,[25] but his mind harbored no evil, for he had safeguarded his thoughts.

11. Now Pythagoras, Diogenes, and Plato drank water, and so did the rest of the army of the would-be philosophers.[26] They even reached such a high degree of vain conceit in their perversion that they ignored God and paid homage to the idols. Those who were in the company of the apostle Peter also made use of wine, and their Teacher,

the Saviour, was Himself reviled for this, when the Jews said: *Why do thy disciples not fast as do those of John?*[27] And again, they attacked the disciples with reviling, saying: *Your Master eats and drinks with publicans and sinners.*[28] It is clear that they would not have attacked them for using bread and water, but only in regard to cooked foods and wine.

12. Again when they were admiring the drinking of water and finding fault with the drinking of wine, the Saviour said: *John came in the way of justice,*[29] *neither eating nor drinking*—clearly meat and wine was meant, for without any eating or drinking he could not have lived—*and they say: He hath a demon. The Son of Man came eating and drinking and they say: Behold a man that is a glutton and a wine drinker, a friend of publicans and sinners,*[30] because of His eating and drinking. Then what shall we do? We shall follow neither those who find fault nor those who give praise, but rather let us fast with John in reasonable fashion even if they say: "They have a devil." Or let us drink wine with Jesus wisely if the body craves it, even if they say: "Behold the gluttons and wine-bibbers."

13. For, to be sure, neither eating nor abstinence is of any account, but it is faith which has extended itself to work done in charity that counts.[31] For whenever faith attends every act, he who eats and drinks according to that faith is uncondemned. *For all that is not of faith is sin.*[32] Whenever any of those sinners says that he participates in faith or does anything else with unreasonable self-confidence and corrupted understanding, the Saviour has given His command: *By their fruits you shall know them.*[33] For it is admitted that the fruits of those who direct their lives

with reason and knowledge according to the godly Apostle are *charity, joy, peace, patience, benignity, goodness, and longanimity.*[34]

14. For Paul himself has said: *But the fruit of the Spirit is*[35] thus and so. He who is eager to obtain such fruits will not eat meat in unreasonable fashion, or aimlessly, or at improper times; nor will he drink wine in those ways; nor will he put up with an evil conscience, for Paul has said that *every one that striveth for the mastery refraineth himself from all things.*[36] Now when one's body is well, one refrains from fattening foods; when one is sick either from pain or grief, or from some misfortune, he will use food or drink as medicine for healing the ailments. He will refrain from things harmful where the soul is concerned—things such as anger, envy, vainglory, torpor,[37] backbiting, and unreasonable suspicion—giving thanks to the Lord.

15. Since I have covered this sufficiently, I shall add another consolation to your love of learning. Avoid as much as is within your ability meeting with men who can be no help to you, those who deck themselves out in unseemly fashion, even if they be orthodox, but especially more so those who are heretical. They only harm you with their hypocrisy, and they seem to be crawling along to a venerable age with their grey hair and wrinkles. For even if you should not be harmed by them, because of your own innate nobility, in lesser vein you will be puffed up and proud and will ridicule them—that much will harm you too. Go to a clear window and seek for meetings with holy men and women so that you may see clearly your own heart as in the case with a book of small writing.[38] The comparison will enable you to see your own sluggishness or indifference.

16. For the appearance of their faces abloom with grey hairs, and the arrangement of their dress, together with their conversation so free from arrogance, and the piety of their language—all this and the grace of their thoughts will increase your strength, even should you be afflicted with spiritual dryness. *The attire of the man and the gait of his feet and the laughter of his teeth show him for what he is,*[39] as Wisdom says.

Now I begin my narrative. I shall leave unmentioned no one in the cities, or in the villages, or in the desert. For we are concerned not with the place where they settled, but rather it is their way of life that we seek.

1. ISIDORE

1. When I first came to Alexandria during the second consulate of Theodosius,[40] the great emperor who now dwells with the angels because of his wonderful faith in Christ, I met a wonderful man in the city. This was the thoroughly accomplished person, Isidore the elder,[41] guest-master of the church of Alexandria, who was reported to have fought the first battles of youth in the desert. I have even seen his cell in the mountain of Nitria.[42] I met him when he was an old man of seventy years and he lived still another fifteen years before his peaceful death.

2. Up to the very end of his life he wore no fine linen except for a headband. He neither bathed[43] nor ate meat. He kept his poor body so well disciplined by grace that all who did not know of his way of life imagined that he lived in luxury. *Time would fail me*[44] were I to attempt a detailed description of his virtues. He was so tender-hearted and peaceful that even his enemies, unbelievers that they were, revered his very shadow because of his great goodness.

3. Such a profound knowledge had he of the Holy Scriptures and the divine teaching that his thoughts were diverted even at the mealtime of the brethren. He became speechless when he was invited to describe the circumstances of his ecstasy. He said: "I went away in thought, snatched up as it were by some vision."

I often knew him to weep at table, and upon asking the reason for the tears, I received this reply: "I am ashamed to partake of irrational food;[45] I am a rational being and I ought to be in a paradise of pleasure because of the power given to us by Christ."

4. He was acquainted with the entire Roman senate and all the wives of the great men when he came first with Athanasius,[46] later with Bishop Demetrius.[47] Very rich and exceedingly generous, he made no will when on the point of death, and he left neither money nor property to his own virgin sisters, but rather entrusted them to Christ,[48] saying: "He who created you will regulate your life as He has ordered mine." There was a band of seventy virgins with his sisters.

5. When I was a young man and visited him, begging to be instructed in the solitary life, I was in my full prime, needing not so much precept as hard bodily toil. He, like a good colt-breaker, led me out of the city to the so-called Solitudes,[49] some five miles out.[50]

2. DOROTHEUS

1. He handed me over to Dorotheus,[51] a Theban ascetic, who had lived sixty years in a cave, and he commanded me to stay three full years with him in subduing my passions. He commanded me to return to him for spiritual training, for he knew the old man passed his life in unremitting discipline. As I fell ill, I could not stay the full time, so I left before the end of three years—his way of life was squalid and harsh.

2. He used to collect stones in the desert all day long in the burning heat along the sea and to build cells for

those who could not build their own, finishing one each year. When I asked him: "What are you doing, Father, killing your body in such heat?" he answered: "It kills me, I will kill it." He would eat six ounces of bread, a bunch of small vegetables, and a proportionate amount of water. God is my witness, I never knew him to stretch out his feet or to sleep on a mat or on a couch, but all night long he would sit up weaving rope of date-palm leaves to earn his food.

3. Having a suspicion that he did this because of me, I inquired about him among his disciples who lived solitary lives, and I found that such had been his way of life from early youth. He had never gone to sleep on purpose, but closed his eyes only when overcome with sleep while at work or eating, so that often a morsel of food would fall from his mouth while he was eating, so drowsy had he become. Once when I was urging him to rest a little while on a rush mat, he said, saddened at heart: "If you persuade the angels to rest, then you can perhaps persuade the eager man."

4. Another time he sent me to his cistern about the ninth hour to fill a jar with water for our refreshment. As I got there I happened to see an asp down in the well and I drew no water, but went back and told him: "We perish, Father;[52] I saw an asp in the well." But he smiled solemnly and looked at me, then shook his head and said: "If the devil sees fit to turn himself into a serpent or a turtle in every well, and falls into our drinking supply, shall you forever remain thirsty?" And he went out and drew water from the same well, and was the first to break his thirst by swallowing. He said: "Where the cross goes, the evil of everything loses ground."[53]

3. POTAMIAENA

1. The aforementioned blessed Isidore[54] had met Antony[55] of sacred memory and told me of an incident well worth recording which he had heard from him. This was about a graceful maiden named Potamiaena,[56] a slave of someone or other during the time of Maximian the persecutor.[57] Her master was unable to seduce her with fervent and oft-repeated arguments.

2. Finally he became enraged and handed her over to the prefect of Alexandria. He denounced her as a Christian and as one who blasphemed the existing state of affairs and the emperors because of the persecutions. He offered him money as a bribe on the condition that "if she agrees to my little game, keep her without punishment"; but should she persist in her rigorous virtue, he asked that she be subjected to all tortures so that she might not survive and ridicule his licentiousness.

3. She was arraigned before the tribunal[58] and the very citadel of her soul was attacked with various instruments of torture, one of these being a great cauldron which the judge ordered filled with pitch and heated. As the pitch was boiling up and on the point of catching fire, he offered her a choice: "Either depart and be subject to the desires of your master, or be assured that I shall order you to be submerged in the cauldron." But she answered him: "May there never be another such judge who orders submission to licentiousness!"

4. Infuriated, he ordered her stripped and cast into the cauldron. But she raised up her voice and cried out: "By the head of the king[59] whom you fear, I beseech you, order me to be slowly submerged into the cauldron, if you really

decide to punish me, so that you may know the endurance which is bestowed upon me by Christ, whom you know not." And being let down little by little over the space of an hour, she died as the boiling pitch reached her neck.

4. DIDYMUS

1. Now a good many of the sainted men and women perfected in the Alexandrian Church were worthy of the land of the meek.[60] Didymus,[61] the blind author,[62] was one of these. I met him four times at various intervals over a period of ten years. He died at the age of eighty-five. He was sightless, having, as he told me, lost his vision at the age of four. Never had he learned to read or attended school.[63]

2. For he had an excellent natural teacher—his own conscience. He was so endowed with the gift of learning that the Scriptures were literally fulfilled in him: *The Lord makes the blind wise*.[64] For he interpreted the Old and the New Testaments word by word, having such regard for doctrine, expounding his explanation so skillfully and firmly, that he surpassed all the ancients in knowledge.

3. Once when he urged me to say a prayer in his cell and I did not comply, he related this incident:[65] "The Blessed Antony entered this cell a third time when visiting me, and when I begged him to pray, he knelt down in the cell to pray at once and did not force me to repeat my invitation, thereby giving me an example of obedience by his compliance. Now, if you are going in the footsteps of his way of life, inasmuch as you are living the life of a

solitary away from home, put aside your contentious spirit."

4. Now he told me this, too: "One day as I was thinking about the life of the miserable Emperor Julian,[66] about his being a persecutor, and I was sorely troubled and had not even tasted my bread up to the time of late evening, because of my thoughts, it so happened that as I sat in my chair I fell asleep and I saw in ecstasy white horses running with soldiers and proclaiming: 'Tell Didymus, Julian died today at the seventh hour; get up and eat,' they said, 'and send word to Athanasius the bishop that he too may know.'[67]

"And I made a note," he said, "of the hour and month and week and day, and it was found to be so."[68]

5. ALEXANDRA

1. He also told me about a maidservant named Alexandra who left the city and immured herself in a tomb. She received the necessities of life through a window and for ten years never looked a woman or man in the face. In the tenth year she fell asleep[69] after she had arranged herself.[70] The woman who used to go to her received no answer and announced this to us. Breaking open the door, we entered and found her asleep.

2. Melania, the thrice blessed, of whom I shall speak later,[71] also told us about her: "I never beheld her face to face, but I stood near the window and asked her to tell why she had immured herself in a tomb. She then told me through the window: 'A man was distracted in mind because of me, and rather than scandalize a soul made in the

image of God, I betook myself alive to a tomb, lest I seem to cause him suffering or reject him.' "

She continued: "When I asked, 'How do you persevere, never seeing anyone, but battling against weariness?'[72] she said: 'From early dawn to the ninth hour I pray from hour to hour while spinning flax. The rest of the time I go over in my mind the holy patriarchs, prophets, apostles, and martyrs. Then I eat my crusts and wait patiently the other hours for my end with good hope.' "

6. THE RICH VIRGIN

1. But I shall not pass over in this narrative those also who lived in vain contempt; this is for the praise of those who lived righteously and for the salvation of those who come across this account.

There was in Alexandria a virgin of humble appearance but of overbearing disposition. She was exceedingly rich, but never gave an obol to a stranger, virgin, church, or poor man. Despite the many rebukes of the fathers, she did not turn herself away from material wealth.

2. Now she had some relatives and she adopted one of them, her sister's daughter, and night and day without any longing for heaven she kept promising her all her wealth. For this is one way the devil deceives us, by contriving to make us fight to excess in the guise of loving one's relatives.

Now it is surely apparent that degrees of relationship make no difference to him who teaches people to commit fratricide, matricide, and patricide.

3. But even if he should seem to enjoin solicitude for relatives, he does not do so out of goodwill towards them,

but to exercise the soul in unrighteousness, knowing the decree: *The unjust shall not possess the kingdom of God.*[73] Now it is possible for a person to be moved by a pious intention and to give help to his relatives, should they be needy, without being contemptuous of his own soul. Whenever one subjects his whole soul to solicitude for a relative, he falls under the law which counts his soul as superfluous.

4. Now this is the way the Psalmist sings of those who fearfully guard their souls: *Who shall ascend into the mountain of the Lord?* (instead of saying it is seldom) *The innocent in hands and clean of heart, who hath not taken his soul in vain.*[74] Those very persons who are neglectful of virtue "take their soul in vain," being of the opinion that the soul is to melt away with the body.

5. Now they say that the blessed Macarius wished to tap a vein[75] of this virgin to alleviate her greed. This Macarius,[76] priest and superior of the poorhouse for cripples, devised the following ruse. In his younger days he had been a worker in stones, what they call a gem engraver. He went to her and said: "Some precious stones, emeralds and hyacinths, have come into my possession; whether they are simply a find or stolen property, I cannot say. Their value has not been ascertained, since they are priceless, but they can be had by anyone who has five hundred coins.

6. "If you take them, you will get your five hundred coins back from one stone; the rest you can use to pretty up your niece."

Intent on his every word, the maiden took the bait and fell at his feet.[77] "I beseech you," she exclaimed, "do not let anyone else have them." Then he invited her: "Come to my house and see them." She was not willing to wait, however, but threw down the five hundred coins for him, saying: "Take them as you wish; for I do not want to see the man who puts them up for sale."

7. He took the five hundred coins and gave them for the needs of the hospital. Some time elapsed, and since the man seemed to have a very great reputation in Alexandria, and a love of God, and was charitable (he was active until he was a hundred; we spent some time with him ourselves), well, she was discreet about reminding him. Eventually she found him in the church and asked him: "I beg you, what did you decide about those stones for which I gave you the five hundred coins?"

8. He said in reply: "Just as soon as you gave me the money I put it down for the price of the stones. If you wish, come and see them in the hospital, for they are there. Come and see if they please you; if they do not, take your money back."

Now the hospital had the women on the upper floor and the men on the ground floor. And leading her he brought her up to the entrance and asked: "What do you want to see first, the hyacinths or the emeralds?"

She replied: "As you please."

9. He took her to the upper floor, pointed out the crippled and inflamed women, and said: "Look, here are your hyacinths!" And he led her back down again and showed her the men: "Behold your emeralds! If they do not please you, take your money back!"

Turning about then, she left, and going back she became ill from much grief, because she had not done this in God's way. Later, when the maid she had been concerned about died childless after marriage, she gave thanks to God.[78]

7. THE MONKS OF NITRIA[79]

1. Now I spent three years in the monasteries in the neighborhood of Alexandria with their some two thousand most noble and zealous inhabitants. Then I left and crossed over to Mount Nitria. Between this mountain and Alexandria there lies a lake called Marea seventy miles long. I was a day and a half crossing this to the mountain on its southern shore.

2. Beyond the mountain stretches the Great Desert reaching as far as Ethiopia, Mazicae, and Mauretania. On the mountain live close to five thousand men following different ways of life, each as he can or will. Thus some live alone, others in pairs, and some in groups. There are seven bakeries on this mountain serving these men as well as the hermits in the Great Desert, six hundred in all.

3. I tarried then for a year on the mountain and was greatly helped by the blessed fathers Arsisius the Great,[80] Poutoubastes,[81] Asius,[82] Cronius,[83] and Sarapion;[84] and as I was spurred on by their many stories about the fathers, I went into the depths of the desert.

On this mountain of Nitria there is a great church in which stand three date palms, each with a whip hanging on it. Now one is for backsliding monks, another for any robbers that attack, the third for any robbers that happen by. All transgressors who are sentenced to a lashing are made fast to a date palm, and are freed when they have received the requisite number of lashes on the back.

4. The guesthouse is close to the church. Here the arriving guest is received until such time as he leaves volun-

tarily. He stays here all the time, even if for a period of two or three years. They allow a guest to remain at leisure for one week; from then on he must help in the garden, bakery, or kitchen. Should he be a noteworthy person, they give him a book, not allowing him to converse with anyone before the sixth hour. On this mountain there are doctors living, and also pastry cooks. They use wine, too, and wine is sold.

5. All these work with their hands at making linen, so that none of them is in want. And indeed, along about the ninth hour one can stand and hear the divine psalmody issuing forth from each cell and imagine one is high above in paradise.[85] They occupy the church on Saturdays and Sundays only. Eight priests have charge of the church; while the senior priest lives, none of the others celebrates or gives the sermon, but they simply sit quietly by him.

6. This Arsisius and many other old men whom we saw with him were contemporaries of Saint Antony. Some among them said they had also known Amoun of Nitria, whose soul Antony saw received and taken up by the angels.[86]

Arsisius said that he also knew Pachomius of Tabennisi,[87] who was prophet and archimandrite[88] of three thousand men; of him I will speak later.

8. AMOUN OF NITRIA

1. He said that this was the way Amoun[89] lived:

He was an orphan and his uncle forced him to marry when he was about twenty-two. Since he was not able to withstand his uncle's pressure, it seemed best to him to be crowned[90] and to take his place in the bridal chamber, and to go through with the whole marriage ceremony. After they had all put the couple on the couch in the bridal chamber and departed, Amoun got up and closed the door. Then sitting down, he called his saintly companion to him and said to her:

2. "Come here, my lady, and I will explain this matter to you. The marriage which we have just gone through is not efficacious. We will do well if henceforth each of us sleeps alone so that we may please God by keeping our virginity intact." And he drew a small book from a fold in his cloak and read to her from the Apostle,[91] from the Saviour Himself as it were, for she could not read. And to most of what he read he added comments from his own mind, and he kept instructing her about chastity and virginity, so that she was convinced by the grace of God and said:

3. "And I, too, am convinced, my lord. What do you now suggest?"

"I propose that from now on each of us live alone."

She would not be content with this, however, and said: "Let us stay in the same house, but in separate beds."

He lived in the same house with her then for eighteen years, putting in his time by day in the garden and balsam plantation, as he was a balsam grower. Balsam grows just like a vine, needing cultivation and pruning, and it requires hard work. In the evenings he would go into the house, say his prayers and eat with her, and then, having said his night prayers, go out.

4. Thus they lived, and both had reached a state of insensibility to lust—the prayers of Amoun availed this. Finally she said to him: "My lord, I have to speak with you.

If you will listen to me, I will be convinced that you love me for God's sake."

He said: "Say what you will."

"It is only this: Since you are a man practicing righteousness, just as I also am eagerly following in your path, let us live separately. It is unspeakable that you hide such virtue as yours living together with me in virginity."

5. He gave praise to God and told her: "Now you keep this house; I shall make another home for myself." And he left and went to the inner mountain of Nitria (there were no monasteries there as yet),[92] and he built himself two rounded cells and lived another twenty-two years in the desert, and died—I should say, rather, that he went to sleep.[93] Twice each year he saw his blessed companion.[94]

6. The blessed Bishop Athanasius told a marvelous thing about this man in his *Life of Antony*.[95] He had come to the Lycos river[96] with his disciple Theodore, and while taking precautions in undressing so that Theodore would not see him naked, he found himself on the opposite bank, carried there by angels without a ferry.[97] In such wise lived Amoun, and so perfect was he that the blessed Antony saw his soul borne aloft by angels. I passed over this river on a ferry with fear in my heart, for it is a canal of the mighty Nile.

9. OR

On this mountain of Nitria was a monk named Or,[98] and the entire brotherhood confirmed his great virtue, and most of all Melania,[99] that "female man of God" who came to the mountain before my time. I never saw him alive myself. In their stories they said that he neither lied, nor swore, nor cursed anyone, nor did he speak unless it was necessary.

10. PAMBO

1. The blessed Pambo[100] also belonged to this mountain. He was the teacher of the four brothers, Dioscorus the bishop, Ammonius, Eusebius, and Euthymius,[101] and also of Origen, the nephew of Dracontius, a marvelous man. Now Pambo was a man of heroic qualities and great superiority, a case in point being that he was one who disdained gold and silver, as the Gospel requires.

2. For the blessed Melania told me this: "When I first came from Rome to Alexandria and heard about his virtue from the blessed Isidore, who showed me the way to him in the desert, I took him a silver coffer containing three hundred pounds of silver and invited him to share in my wealth. He was sitting weaving palm leaves, and he merely blessed me and said: 'May God reward you!'

3. "And he told his steward Origen: 'Take this and dispense it to all the brethren down in Libya and on the islands, for those monasteries are in greater need.' He gave him orders not to dispense any of it in Egypt because that country was better off."

She continued: "I was standing by and expecting to be honored or praised by him for my donation, but I heard nothing from him, and so I spoke up to him: 'So you may know, O lord, how much it is, there are three hundred pounds.'

4. "He did not so much as raise his head, but said: 'My child, He who measures the mountains[102] knows better the amount of the silver. If you were giving it to me, you

spoke well; but if you are giving it to God, who did not overlook the two obols,[103] then be quiet.'

"Thus," she said, "did the Lord show His power when I went to the mountain.

5. "Shortly afterward this man of God fell asleep, not consumed by a fever or any sickness, but in the act of stitching a basket when he was seventy years old. He had sent for me, and when he was ready to make the last stitch and was on the point of departing, he said to me: 'Take this basket from my hands that you may remember me, for I have nothing else I might leave you.' "

Then she prepared him for burial by winding his body in linen cloths. She buried him and then withdrew from the desert, and she kept the basket with her until her death.

6. When this Pambo was dying he is reported to have said this to Origen, the priest and steward, and to Ammonius—famous men they were—and to the rest of the brethren who were present just as he was about to depart: "From the time when I came into the desert here and built my cell and dwelt here, I do not recall having eaten *bread for nothing*,[104] but only that which was the work of my own hands. Nor do I repent of any word I have spoken up to now; and thus I go to God as one who has not even begun to serve Him."

7. Origen and Ammonius bore additional witness by telling us this: When asked about a scriptural phrase or some other problem, he would never answer on the spur of the moment, but used to say: "I have not found it." Often a period of three months would go by and he had not given an answer, saying that he had not comprehended it. So they accepted his answers as though they were from God Himself, approved and shaped by His will. He is

said to have excelled even the great Antony and others in this virtue, namely, accuracy of speech.

8. This incident is related about Pambo: Pior[105] the ascetic came to him and brought his own bread. When he was reprimanded and asked: "Why did you do this?" he answered: "So that I need not bother you." Pambo taught him a silent lesson very forcefully. He later went to see Pior and took along with him some moistened bread. When asked for an explanation, he said: "I moistened it, too, so I would not bother you."

11. AMMONIUS

1. This Ammonius[106] who was a student of Pambo attained the heights of piety along with his three brothers and two sisters. They went down to the desert, each living separately and keeping a distance from the others. Now since the man was a very learned scholar,[107] a certain city eagerly sought him with the object of making him bishop. The people approached the blessed Timotheus,[108] begging him to appoint Ammonius as their bishop.

2. He said to them: "Bring him to me and I will ordain him."

Then they went with envoys and Ammonius saw that he was trapped. He pleaded with them and solemnly swore that he would not accept the election, that he would not leave the desert. They did not give in to him. Then while they were looking on he took a pair of shears and cut off his left ear,[109] right back to the head, and he said: "And from now on be assured that it is impossible for me, as the law forbids a man with his ear cut off to be ordained priest."[110]

3. So they let him go and left. They went back and told the bishop, who said to them: "Let this law be kept by the Jews. If you bring me a man with his nose cut off, but worthy in other respects, I will ordain him."

So they left again and begged Ammonius, who swore to them: "If you compel me, I will cut out my tongue." And so they let him go and went away.

4. The following marvel is told about this Ammonius: He never pampered his flesh when desire rose up in revolt, but he heated an iron in the fire and applied it to his limbs, so that he became ulcerated all over. From his youth to death his fare consisted of raw foods only; he ate nothing prepared with fire except bread. He had committed to memory the Old and New Testaments, and he knew by heart 6,000,000 verses[111] of the highly reputable writings of Origen,[112] Didymus,[113] Pierius, and Stephen,[114] so the fathers of the desert testify.

5. If anyone at all was a guide to the brethren in the desert, he was one. The blessed Evagrius,[115] an inspired and penetrating man, gave him this stamp of approval: "I have never seen a man more free from passion than he was."

[When he had to go on a trip to Constantinople, he fell asleep after a short time and was buried in the martyr's shrine called Rufinianae. It is said that his tomb cures all who suffer from shivering spells.][116]

12. BENJAMIN

1. In this mountain at Nitria there was a man named Benjamin[117] who had lived eighty years and attained the height of ascetic perfection. He was deemed worthy of

the gift of healing, so that every one on whom he laid his hands, or whom he blessed and gave oil,[118] was cured of all sickness. Now this man, so greatly honored by the gift of healing, contracted dropsy about eight months before he died. His body swelled up to such a size that he seemed to be another Job.[119] So Dioscorus the bishop,[120] at that time the priest of Mount Nitria, took both the blessed Evagrius and me aside and said:

2. "Come here, see a new Job who possesses boundless gratitude while in a state of great bodily swelling and incurable sickness."[121]

So we went and saw his body so greatly swollen that another person's fingers could not reach around one of his. Unable to look any longer at the terrible suffering, we turned our eyes aside. Then that blessed Benjamin spoke to us: "Pray, my children, that the inner man not contract dropsy; for this body did not help me when it was well, nor has it caused me harm when faring badly."

3. For eight months, then, a very wide seat was set out for him on which he sat all the time. He was no longer able to lie down, because of other needs. Even in this great sickness he cured others. I felt that I must tell about this sickness so that we might not be too surprised when some accident befalls just men. When he died, the door and jambs were pulled down so that his body could be carried out of the house, so great was the swelling.[122]

13. APOLLONIUS

1. There was a businessman named Apollonius[123] who had renounced the world and lived on Mount Nitria. As he was too advanced in years to learn a craft or to work as

a scribe,[124] he lived on the mountain for twenty years engaged in this business: with his own money and his own efforts he would buy all kinds of medicines and groceries at Alexandria and provide for all the brethren in their sicknesses.

2. He could be seen making his rounds of the monasteries from early morn to the ninth hour, going in door after door to find out if any one was sick. He used to bring grapes, pomegranates, eggs, and cakes such as the sick fancy, and he found this a very profitable livelihood[125] in his old age. When he died he left his wares to one just like himself, and he encouraged him to carry on with this service. For there were five thousand monks living on the mountain, and there was a need for this visiting, since the place was a desert.[126]

14. PAESIUS AND ISAIAS

1. Also there were Paesius and Isaias,[127] sons of a Spanish merchant. When their father died, they divided the estate they held, namely five thousand coins, clothes, and slaves. They deliberated and planned together: "Brother, what kind of life shall we lead? If we become merchants, such as our father was, we will still be entrusting our work to others.

2. "Then we would risk harm at the hands of pirates on the high seas. Come, let us take up the monastic life so that we may profit by our father's goods and still not lose our souls."

The prospect of monastic life pleased them, but they found themselves in disagreement. For when they had divided the property, they each had in mind to please God, but by taking different ways of life.

3. Now the one shared everything among the monasteries, churches, and prisons; he learned a trade so that he might provide bread for himself and he spent his time at ascetic practices and prayer. The other, however, made no distribution of his share, but built a monastery for himself and took in a few brethren. Then he took in every stranger, every invalid, every old man, and every poor one as well, setting up three or four tables every Saturday and Sunday. In this way he spent his money.

4. After they both were dead, various pronouncements were made about them as though they had both been perfect. Some preferred one, some the other. Then rivalry developed among the brethren in regard to the eulogies. They went to the blessed Pambo and entrusted the judgment to him, thinking to learn from him which was the better way of life. He told them: "Both were perfect. One showed the work of Abraham; the other, that of Elias."[128]

5. One faction said: "By your feet, we implore you, how can they be equal?" And this group considered the ascetic the greater, and insisted that he did what the Gospel commended,[129] selling all and giving to the poor, and every hour both day and night carried the cross and followed the Saviour even in his prayers.[130] But the others argued heatedly, saying that Isaias had shared everything with the needy and even used to sit on the highways and gather together the oppressed. Not only did he relieve his own soul, but many others as well by tending the sick and helping them.

6. Pambo told them: "Again I say to you, they are both equal. I firmly insist to each of you that the one, if he had

not lived so ascetically, would not be worthy to be compared with the goodness of the other. As for the other, he refreshed strangers, and thereby himself as well, and even if he appeared to carry the load of toil, he had also its relief thereafter. Wait until I have a revelation from God, and then come back and learn it."

They returned some days later and he told them: "I saw both of them standing in paradise in the presence of God."

15. MACARIUS THE YOUNGER

1. A young man named Macarius[131] about eighteen years of age was playing with his comrades along Lake Marea.[132] He was pasturing animals and accidentally killed someone. Telling no one about it, he went off to the desert; he was so afraid of God and of man that he had no regard for himself, and he stayed in the desert for three years without a shelter. Now the land is rainless, as everyone knows either by hearsay or by direct experience.

2. Afterwards he built himself a cell and lived another twenty-five years there. He was deemed worthy of the gift of spitting upon demons,[133] and he rejoiced in his solitude. I spent quite some time with him, and I asked him how he felt about his sin of homicide. He said that it was far from his thoughts, and that he even rejoiced in it, since it was actually the starting point of his salvation.

3. He said, bringing testimony from Holy Writ, that Moses would not have been deemed worthy of the divine vision and the great gift of writing inspired words if he had not fled to Mount Sinai in fear of Pharaoh, because of the homicide he had committed in Egypt.[134] I do not say this to make light of homicide, but rather to show that

there are virtues which are due to circumstances, when a man does not advance to good of himself. For some virtues are deliberately chosen and others are dependent upon circumstances.

16. NATHANIEL

1. Another of the old men was one called Nathaniel.[135] I never met him in the flesh, for he had gone to sleep[136] some fifteen years before my visit. Now when I met with those who had practiced asceticism with him and were indeed his contemporaries, I busied myself to ask about the virtue of this man. They showed me his cell; no one lives there any more, because it is too close to civilization. He had built it when the anchorites were few and far between. They said about him that one of his peculiarities was that he stayed so much in his cell, in order that he might not weaken in his resolution.

2. From the very beginning he was made sport of by the demon who mocks and deceives everyone. He seemed to feel bored at the first cell, so he went off and built another one closer to the city. After he had finished it and lived there for three or four months, the demon happened by at night holding a rawhide just as public executioners do. He had the appearance of a ragged soldier and he made noises with the rawhide. The blessed Nathaniel replied to this, saying: "Who are you, carrying on like this in my lodging?"

The demon answered: "I am the same one who drove you away from the other cell. I have come now to drive you out of this one, too."

3. Nathaniel knew that he had been fooled, and he

turned back again to his first cell. And to spite the demon, he did not cross the portal for fully thirty-seven years. The demon showed him all sorts of things, having in mind to force him out. This was one of his ruses: He waited for the visit of seven holy bishops and—whether this happened through God's foresight or the demon's own temptation—nearly drove Nathaniel from his purpose. For when the bishops were departing after prayer, Nathaniel did not march with them a single step.

4. The deacons told him: "You are committing an arrogant act, Father, not escorting the bishops forth."

But he said: "I am dead both to my sovereign bishops and to the whole world. I have an intention which is hidden, and God knows my heart, why I do not escort them forth."

The demon had failed in this effort, and about nine months before Nathaniel's death he took on the shape of a boy[137] about ten driving an ass carrying a basket of bread. It was late in the evening when he came up to Nathaniel's cell and he pretended that the ass had fallen down and the boy was crying out:

5. "Father Nathaniel, have mercy on me and give me a hand!"

Nathaniel heard the voice of the make-believe boy and opened the door. Standing inside, he asked him: "Who are you and what do you want me to do?"

"I am So-and-so's servant," he said, "and I am bringing loaves because tomorrow is this brother's agape,[138] and at dawn offerings will be needed. I beg you, do not neglect me, lest I be eaten by the hyenas. There are many hyenas around here."

The blessed Nathaniel stood there surprised and

stunned; filled with compassion, he debated within himself and said: "I must fail either the commandment or my resolution."[139]

6. After reflecting that it would be better for the confusion of the devil not to shake the resolution of so many years, he prayed, and he spoke to the make-believe boy who had addressed him: "Listen, boy! I believe that if you are in need, the God whom I serve will send you aid, and no hyenas, or anything else, will cause you any harm. But if you are a temptation, God will reveal the whole business here." He shut the door and went in.

The demon was confounded at this defeat and dissolved into a storm and into wild asses galloping off and kicking up stones.[140]

Such was the contest of the blessed Nathaniel, and this was his manner of life, and such was his end.

17. MACARIUS OF EGYPT

1. I am reluctant to speak or to write of the many great and almost unbelievable events involving the Macarii,[141] those famous men, lest I be accounted a liar. For the Lord *shall destroy all that speak a lie*,[142] as the Holy Spirit declared. Indeed, I am not lying, most trusted one, believe me! Of the two Macarii, one was Egyptian by race, the other, the one who sold sweetmeats, was of Alexandria.

2. First I shall tell about the Egyptian,[143] who lived all of ninety years. Sixty of these he spent in the desert, having gone there when a young man of thirty. He was deemed worthy of such discernment that he was called the "young-old man." And because of this he made the greater progress. By the time he was forty he received the gift of

fighting spirits and of prophecy. He was even deemed worthy of the priesthood.

3. There were two disciples with him in the inner desert which is called Scete.[144] One of them remained close to him because of the number who came to be healed, while the other stayed in a cell near by. After some time had passed and he saw clearly with clairvoyant eye what the future held in store, he told his attendant, the one whose name was John, who later became a priest in his own place: "Listen to me, brother John, and heed my warning. You are being tempted, and it is the spirit of avarice that is tempting you.

4. "For I have seen this, and I know that if you are patient with me, you will be perfected here and glorified, *nor shall the scourge come near thy dwelling*,[145] but if you do not listen to me, the end of Gieza, whose sickness you now suffer, shall come on you."[146]

Now it so happened that this John was disobedient after the death of Macarius. Then another fifteen or twenty years later, when he had robbed the poor, he came down with elephantiasis; you could not put a finger on a single part of his body without its being contaminated. This then was the prophecy of the saintly Macarius.

5. Now as regards the partaking of food and drink, it would be pointless to go into detail, since even among the easygoing in these parts one cannot find gluttony or indifference. This was because of the dearth of necessities and the fervor of the inhabitants.

And now I will speak of the rest of his asceticism, for he was said to be in continual ecstasy. He occupied himself much more with God than with earthly things, and these are the wonders told of him:

6. An Egyptian, deeply enamored of a married woman of good position, was not able to entice her. He consulted a sorcerer and said: "Get her to love me, or cause her husband to throw her out." The sorcerer received a goodly sum of money, used magical charms, and caused her to assume the shape of a brood mare. The husband came in and was astonished to see a mare lying on the bed. He cried and wept. He talked to the beast. No sort of reply was forthcoming. He called on the priests of the village.

7. He brought them in and showed them. No solution was found. For three days she neither ate fodder as a mare nor ate bread as a human, but was deprived of both types of food. At last, so that God might be praised and the virtue of the holy Macarius be made manifest, it entered into the mind of the husband to lead her out into the desert. He bridled her like a horse and led her away to the desert. The brethren stood by the cell of Macarius to contend with her husband when they drew near, and they asked:

8. "Why did you drive this mare here?"

He said: "That she may receive mercy."

They asked: "What ails her?"

Her husband answered: "She was my wife and was changed into a horse, and today is the third day she has not tasted a thing."

They told this to the saint who was at prayer within, for God had revealed this to him and he was praying for her. Then the holy Macarius spoke to them: "You are the horses, for you have the eyes of horses.

9. "Now she is a woman, not at all changed, except in the eyes of self-deceived men."

And he blessed water, poured it on her bare skin from the head downward, and made her appear as a woman. He gave her food then and made her eat, and he sent her away with her husband, giving thanks to the Lord. And he enjoined her never to neglect the Church or stay away from Communion. "These things happened to you because you were not at the Mysteries for five weeks."[147]

10. This is another of his ascetic acts: Over a long period of time he made a tunnel under the earth from his cell for about half a mile and a cave at the end. Whenever too many people crowded in on him, he would secretly leave his cell and go to the cave, and no one would find him. One of his earnest disciples told us this and added that on his way to the cave he recited twenty-four prayers, and on his way back, twenty-four more.

11. A report went about concerning him that he had brought a dead person to life to convince a heretic who did not believe in the resurrection of the body.[148] And this report prevailed in the desert. Once a young man who had a demon was brought by his weeping mother to Macarius. He was tied to two men. And this was how the demon acted: After downing three bushels of bread and a Cilician jar of water, he would retch out the food and vaporize it. In this way both food and drink were as it were consumed by fire.

12. For there is a class of demons called fiery,[149] since demons have differences just as men do, not of essence but of knowledge. Now this young man did not have enough food from his own mother, so he ate his own excrement —often he even drank his own water. As his mother was weeping and beseeching the saint, Macarius took the young man and prayed for him, invoking God. And after one or two days, when the fever had abated, blessed Macarius asked her:

13. "How much would you have him eat?"

She answered: "Ten pounds of bread."

Then he censured her on the grounds that this was too much. He prayed over the young man and fasted for the space of seven days; then he put the young man on a diet of three pounds and obliged him to do some work. Thus cured, the young man was brought back to his mother.

And this wonder God accomplished through Macarius. I did not meet him, since he had fallen asleep a year before I entered the desert.

18. MACARIUS OF ALEXANDRIA

1. I met the other Macarius,[150] however, the one from Alexandria, a priest of so-called Cellia,[151] where I stayed for nine years,[152] and he was actually alive during three of those years. Some of the things I saw, others I heard about, and some I had by hearsay from others.

Such was his practice that whenever he heard of any asceticism, he surpassed it to perfection.[153] He heard from some that the Tabennesiote monks eat their food un-cooked throughout the Lenten period, so he made up his mind to eat no food that had come in contact with fire. For seven years he partook of nothing but raw vegetables, if these could be found, with a little moistened pulse.

2. He brought this virtue to perfection, and then heard about some other monk who ate but a pound of bread a day.[154] He broke up his ration-biscuit[155] into small bits, and put it into a measuring jar, and determined to eat only as much as his hand brought up. And he used to say jok-ingly: "I would take hold of quite a few morsels, but could not take them all out because of the narrow neck;

for just like a toll-collector, it would not let me pass." He kept this up for three years, eating about four or five ounces and drinking about the equivalent amount of water, and a pint of olive oil lasted him a year.

3. Here is another example of his asceticism: He decided to be above the need for sleep, and he claimed that he did not go under a roof for twenty days in order to conquer sleep. He was burned by the heat of the sun and was drawn up with the cold at night. And he also said: "If I had not gone into the house and obtained the advantage of some sleep, my brain would have shriveled up for good. I conquered to the extent I was able, but I gave in to the extent my nature required sleep."

4. Early one morning when he was sitting in his cell a gnat stung him on the foot.[156] Feeling the pain, he killed it with his hands, and it was gorged with his blood. He accused himself of acting out of revenge and he condemned himself to sit naked in the marsh of Scete out in the great desert for a period of six months. Here the mosquitoes lacerate even the hides of the wild swine just as wasps do. Soon he was bitten all over his body, and he became so swollen that some thought he had elephantiasis. When he returned to his cell after six months he was recognized as Macarius only by his voice.

5. He once wished, so he told us, to enter the garden-tomb of Jannes and Jambres.[157] Now this garden-tomb had belonged to the magicians who had power along with Pharaoh back in the old days.[158] Since they held power for a long time they built the work with stones four feet square. They erected their monument there and put away much gold. They even planted trees there, for the spot was damp, and they dug a well, too.

6. Since the holy man did not know the road, he followed the stars, traversing the desert as though it were the sea.[159] Taking a bundle of reeds, he placed one at every mile, leaving a mark so that he might find the way back on his return. After traveling for nine days, he reached the place. Then the demon who ever acts in opposition to the athletes of Christ[160] collected all the reeds and put them by his head as he slept near the garden-tomb.

7. He found the reeds upon arising. God had permitted this for his own further training, so that he might not place trust in reeds, but rather in the pillar of cloud[161] that led Israel for forty years in the desert. He used to say: "Seventy demons rushed from the garden-tomb to meet me, shouting and fluttering like crows in front of me, saying: 'What do you wish, Macarius? What do you want, monk? Why did you come to our place? You cannot stay here.' I told them," he said, " 'Let me but go in and look about, and then leave.' "

8. He continued: "Upon entering, I found a hanging brass jar and an iron chain near the well, already consumed by time; the pomegranates had nothing inside, so dried out were they by the sun."

Then he started back, and was twenty days traveling. When the water which he was carrying gave out, and also the bread, he was in a very precarious situation. And just when he was on the verge of collapse, he caught sight of a maiden dressed in a pure white linen robe and holding a jug dripping water.

9. He said that she was far off, about a stade or two, and he was on the journey three days seeing her with the jug, standing there as it were, but he was unable to attain it, as in a dream. He survived only in hopes of drinking it.

Next there appeared a herd of antelope. One of them had a calf, and he saw that her udder was dripping milk. Crawling under her, he sucked and was refreshed. The antelope accompanied him to his cell and nursed him, but would not take her own calf.

10. Once he was digging a well close to some vegetable shoots and an asp (this is a poisonous animal) bit him. He took it in his two hands by the lips and tore it apart, saying: "If God did not send you, how did you dare come?"[162]

He had various cells in the desert—one at Scete in the innermost part of the Great Desert, another in Libya, one in so-called Cellia, and still another at Mount Nitria. Some of these were windowless, and he is said to have sat in them in darkness during Lent; another was too narrow for him to stretch out his feet in it; another was more commodious, and in this one he met those who visited him.

11. He cured so many demon-ridden people that numbers fail. When I was there a virgin was brought from Thessalonica, a noble woman who had been suffering from paralysis for a good many years. He anointed her for twenty days with holy oil[163] with his own hands while praying over her, and he sent her away sound and healthy. After she had gone away, she sent him gifts of fruit.

12. He heard that the Tabennesiotes had a great way of life; he changed his clothes, assumed the appearance of a laborer, and traveled for fifteen days into the Thebaid, going through the desert. Arriving at the monastery of Tabennisi, he sought out their archimandrite Pachomius,[164] a most worthy man who had the gift of prophecy. This latter did not know Macarius, who upon meeting him said: "I beg you, receive me into your hermitage that I may become a monk."

13. Pachomius said to him: "You come here already an old man;[165] you cannot practice the ascetic life. The brethren are ascetics and you cannot bear their labors; you will be embarrassed and leave, and will revile them." Nor did he receive him on the first day or the second, but not until the seventh day.

After he had stood his ground with perseverance and in fasting, he said: "Receive me, Father;[166] if I do not fast and work along with them, order me to be expelled."

He persuaded the brethren to admit him.[167] The establishment at this time consisted of fourteen hundred men.[168]

14. Shortly after he entered, Lent started, and he saw each one practicing a different kind of asceticism.[169] One ate only at evening, another only every other day, another only every five days—this one remained standing all night, but sat by day. Macarius moistened a great many palm leaves and he stood in a corner until the forty days were over and it was Easter. He ate no bread and drank no water, nor did he bend his knee or lie down. He partook of nothing but a few cabbage leaves, and that on Sunday, so that he might at least give the appearance of eating.

15. And whenever he went out for his own need, he came back quickly and stood there, speaking to no one, not opening his mouth, but standing in silence. Except for the prayer in his heart and the palm leaves in his hands, he did nothing. All of them saw this and quarreled with the superior and said: "Where did you get this bodiless man for our condemnation? Either throw him out or know that we are all leaving."

Having noticed his way of life, Pachomius prayed to God that it might be revealed to him who this might be.

16. Then it was revealed to him. Taking Macarius by the hand, he led him into the oratory where the altar was and said to him: "Come, Reverend,[170] you are Macarius, and you have concealed this from me. I have desired for many years to meet you. I am grateful to you for having made my children[171] knuckle down so that they might not become haughty about their own ascetic practices. Go away now to your own place, for you have stayed long enough with us. And pray for us, too."

He left them as requested.

17. At another time he told us this: "I had succeeded well in every kind of life I desired; then I wanted still something else, namely, to keep my mind fixed upon God without any distractions for the space of but five days. I decided upon this and shut up my cell and the hall so as to answer no man, and I began my stand at the second hour. I gave these orders to my mind: 'Do not descend from heaven, for there you have angels, archangels, the powers above, the God of all of us; only do not descend from heaven.'

18. "And I endured this for two days and nights, so that I irritated the demon and he became a fiery flame and burned up everything of mine that was in the cell. Even the rush mat I stood on was burned up by the fire. I even thought that I was on fire. Finally, overwhelmed by fear, I left on the third day, unable to keep my mind free from distraction. I came down to view the world lest I be thought arrogant."

19. Once when I approached this holy Macarius I found lying outside his cell a priest of the village whose head was all eaten away by the disease of cancer. The very bone on the top of his head was visible. He had come to

be cured and Macarius had not received him. I called to Macarius and said: "I beg of you, be merciful to him and give him an answer."

20. And he replied to me: "He is not worthy to be cured. This was sent to him as a good lesson. If you want him cured, persuade him to refrain from saying the Mass; for he was both indulging his lust and exercising the priestly function, and for this he is receiving this lesson, and God is healing him."

When I told the afflicted man this, he agreed, and he vowed that he would no longer exercise the priestly function. Then Macarius received him, saying: "Do you believe that God exists?"

He answered: "I do believe."

21. "Were you able to ridicule God?"

"No," he replied.

"If you realize your sin and understand the lesson you have received from God, amend your ways for the future."

He confessed his sin and promised to sin no more, and not to officiate in church, but to embrace the lay state. And so Macarius laid his hand on him, and in a few days he was cured. Hair grew back on his head and he went away cured.

22. Before my very eyes a young boy possessed by an evil spirit was brought to him. He put one hand on his head and the other over his heart, and he prayed so intently that he caused the boy to be suspended in the air. The boy swelled up like a wineskin and became so inflamed that he became afflicted with erysipelas. Suddenly crying out he emitted water through all his sense organs, and he returned once more to his former size. Macarius

handed him back to his father then, after anointing the boy with holy oil and pouring water on him. He enjoined him not to partake of meat or wine for forty days, and thus he cured him.

23. At one time schemes of vainglory troubled him, throwing him out of his cell and suggesting that he go to Rome to promote the designs of Providence by curing the sick—for grace against spirits worked strongly in him. And as he did not take heed for a while, but was strongly pressed, he fell on the threshold of his cell, put his feet outside, and said: "Pull me and drag me, O demons, I shall not go on my feet. If you can drag me, then I shall go." He declared on oath: "I will lie here until evening. If you do not shake me, I will not listen."

24. He lay there quite a while and then got up. As night came on, demons attacked him again; but he filled up a basket with two measures of sand, put it upon his shoulders, and shuffled about the desert. Theosebius the Sweeper, he of Antioch born, came across him and addressed him: "What are you carrying, Father? Hand the load over to me and do not be bothered with it." He replied: "I am molesting my tempter; he is uncontrollable and tries to throw me out." When he had shuffled about for a long time, he went into his cell, his body having been beaten into subjection.

25. This holy Macarius told me this also, for he was a priest:[172] "I had noticed that at the time of the distribution of the Mysteries I never gave the Sacrament to Mark the ascetic, but rather an angel administered to him from the altar. I saw only the wrist of the minister's hand." This Mark was a young man who knew by heart the Old and

the New Testaments; he was as gentle as can be and most reserved.

26. One day in a leisurely mood I went and sat near the door of the old man, who was then very advanced in age. I was thinking of him as over and above men in years, and I listened to him talking and moving about. And there he was inside, all alone, well on to a hundred and with his teeth all gone, fighting both himself and the devil, saying: "What do you want, you old man of evil? Look, you have had oil and wine—what more can you want, you grey-haired old glutton?" Thus he scolded himself. Then a word for the devil, too (for he must have his due): "Do I still owe you anything? You will find nothing! Depart from me!" And, as though humming, he kept saying to himself: "Come, you white-haired old glutton, *how long shall I be with you?*"[173]

27. Paphnutius, a disciple of his, told us that one day a hyena[174] brought a blind pup of hers to Macarius. She knocked with her head at the door of the hall, went inside, and cast the young pup at his feet. He took it up and put spittle on its eyes, and then prayed. *Immediately it saw the light.*[175] The mother suckled it, picked it up, and left.

28. The next day she brought him[176] the hide of a large sheep. The blessed Melania told me: "I took that fleece as a visiting-gift."

And what is so remarkable about this, that He who subdued the lions for Daniel[177] should also enlighten the hyena?

And he said that from the time that he was baptized he did not spit on the ground,[178] and it was then sixty years since he had been baptized.

29. As for his appearance, he was slight and without a beard, having hair only about the lips and at the end of the chin, for the asceticism he practiced did not allow hair to sprout on him. I went to him once, bored with weariness, and said: "What shall I do, Father, since my thoughts prompt me to leave, seeing I have made no progress here?" And he told me: "Tell them on Christ's behalf, I am holding up the walls here."[179]

These were a few of many tales of the holy Macarius.[180]

19. MOSES THE ETHIOPIAN[181]

1. There was a certain Moses,[182] a black Ethiopian, who served as houseman to some official in the administration. His master discharged him for exasperating behavior and for stealing; he was thought even to have committed murder. I am forced to tell about his knavery in order to show the virtue of his conversion. At any rate, they said that he had been head of a robber-gang, and the principal story of his stealing episodes was one in which he bore a grudge against a shepherd who one night stood between him and his objective with his dogs.

2. Desiring to kill the shepherd, he searched for the place where he kept the sheep. He was notified that it was across the Nile. The river was then in full flood and at least a mile across, so he put his sword between his teeth, placed his cloak on his head, plunged into the river, and swam to the other side. While he was swimming across the river, the shepherd was able to escape by burying himself in the sand. Well, he selected and killed four rams, tied them together with a cord, and swam back again.

3. He came to a small slaughtering place and skinned

them. Then he ate the best part of the meat and sold the sheepskins to buy wine. He then drank off a measure of wine, equal to eighteen Italian pints, and went off fifty miles to where he had his band. Late in the day he was brought to his senses by some circumstance and he betook himself to a monastery. After his conversion he behaved in such fashion that he brought even his companion in evil, the demon[183] who had been with him from his youth, to open recognition of Christ.

Among other things, this, too, is told of him: Four robbers not knowing who he was fell upon him in his cell.

4. He tied them all together like a package,[184] put them on his back like a bundle of straw, and took them to the church of the brethren. "Since I may not hurt anyone," he said, "what do you want me to do with these?"

The robbers confessed and knew that he was Moses, the onetime notorious and well-known robber. They glorified God and spurned the world because of his conversion. For they reasoned thus: "If he who was such a strong and powerful thief fears God, why should we put off our own salvation?"

5. Then demons attacked this Moses, trying to draw him back into his old ways of intemperance and impurity. He was tempted to such an extent, so he told us, that he nearly failed in his resolution. Then he went to the great Isidore, I mean the one in Scete,[185] and related all the details of the contest to him.

Isidore said: "Do not become discouraged. These were the beginnings, and for this reason they were the more severe as they attacked, since they were testing your character.

6. "A dog does not by nature stay away from a meat

market, but only if the market is closed up and no one gives him anything does he stop coming by.[186] So also in your case. If you stand firm, the demon will have to leave you in discouragement."

He went back then, and from that hour he practiced asceticism more zealously, and especially in regard to food. He partook of nothing but dry bread, meanwhile carrying a full burden and saying fifty prayers daily. He mortified his poor body, but continued to be consumed by fire and troubled by dreams.

7. Once more he went to another of the saints and asked him: "What shall I do, since dreams of my mind blind my reason because of my customary illicit pleasures?" He was told: "You have not withdrawn your mind from these images and for that reason you are undergoing this. Give yourself over to vigils, pray and fast, and soon you will be rid of them."

He listened to this advice, went back to his cell, and pledged that throughout the night he would not lie down or even bend his knees.

8. He stayed in his cell six years then, standing in the middle of his cell every night praying, never shutting his eyes—and still he could not control his mind. He started another way of life. Each night he went out to the cells of the old men and the more ascetic of them, and he took their water pitchers and kept them filled without their knowledge. For they have their water a good way off— some two miles, others five, and some only half a mile.

9. One night the demon was lying in wait for him and lost his patience. When Moses was bending over at the well, the demon gave him a blow across his loins with a cudgel and left him as one who was dead, who neither felt

anything nor knew what had happened. The next day someone came to draw water and found him lying there and told the great Isidore, the priest of Scete. He took him to the church and he was ill for a year, so that his body and soul scarcely regained strength.

10. The great Isidore said then: "Stop contending with demons and do not bother them, for there are limits in bravery as well as in ascetic practice."

He replied: "I shall not stop before my fantasy of demons ceases."

Isidore said: "In the name of Jesus Christ, your dreams have vanished. Now receive Communion confidently.[187] You were subjected to this for your own good, so that you might not boast of overcoming passion."

11. And he went back to his own cell again. Later, after about two months, he was asked by the great Isidore and he said he no longer suffered anything. He was deemed worthy of power over demons; we have a greater fear of flies than he had of demons.

Such was the life of Moses the Ethiopian; so he, too, was accounted one of the great ones of the fathers. He died in Scete as a priest seventy-five years old, leaving seventy pupils.

20. PAUL

1. There is in Egypt a mountain called Pherme,[188] on the border of the desert of Scete. Here on this mountain live about five hundred monks, ascetics all. Among them there was a certain Paul[189] who led this sort of life: He engaged in no work or business, and he took nothing except what he ate. Now his work and asceticism amounted

to continual prayer. For he knew three hundred prayers by heart, and he would collect that many pebbles, hold them in his lap, and at each prayer cast out a pebble.[190]

2. He went to meet the holy Macarius, the one they called "the Citizen,"[191] and said to him: "Father Macarius, I am dejected!" When Macarius enjoined him to tell the cause of this, he said: "In a certain village there lives a virgin who has practiced asceticism for thirty years. They say that she eats nothing except on Saturday and Sunday.[192] But in the whole period of five days she spends between eating, she says seven hundred prayers. And I felt sorry for myself when I learned of that, because I cannot say more than three hundred."

3. The blessed Macarius answered him: "I am sixty years old and I say one hundred prayers daily. I support myself besides, and I give time for consultations with the brethren, and my reason tells me that I am not negligent. But if you say three hundred prayers and your reason bothers you, it is clear that you do not say them with simplicity of heart, or else you could say more and do not."

21. EULOGIUS AND THE CRIPPLE

1. Cronius,[193] the priest of Nitria, told me this one: "When I was rather young and fled from the monastery of my archimandrite because of tedium, I came in my wandering as far as the mountain of Saint Antony.[194] The place lay between Babylon[195] and Heraclea[196] against the Great Desert, which stretches to the Red Sea about thirty miles from the river. When I arrived at his monastery by the river where dwelt his two disciples at Pispir,[197] namely

Macarius and Amatas,[198] they who buried him, I waited five days in order to meet Saint Antony.

2. "Now he was said to direct his course to this monastery sometimes every ten days, again every twenty days, sometimes as often as every five days, as God directed him, to accomplish good for those who happened to come to the monastery. Different brothers gathered there with different needs.[199] Among them were a certain Eulogius, an Alexandrian solitary, and a cripple, and the reason they had come was this:

3. "This Eulogius, who was, moreover, well educated in the humanities[200] and inspired with a love of immortality, had parted with the excitement of the world and disposed of everything, keeping out a little money for himself, as he was not able to work. Bored with himself, and not wishing to enter a community, he had found someone lying at the market place, a cripple who had neither feet nor hands—only his tongue was still functioning and served as a contact with passers-by.

4. "Well, Eulogius stood and looked intently at him, and he prayed to God and made a compact with Him: 'Lord, in your name I will take this crippled man and look after him until death, so that I may be saved through him. Graciously grant me to endure this undertaking.'

"And he approached the cripple and said to him: 'Would you like me, sir, to take you into my house and take care of you?'

"He replied: 'Certainly I would.'

" 'Well, I will fetch my mule and take you.'

"It was agreed. He brought the mule, took him to his guestchamber, and looked after him.[201]

5. "The cripple lived then for fifteen years under his

care. Eulogius with his own hands washed and looked after him as his needs required. Now after fifteen years a demon assailed the cripple and he turned against Eulogius. He proceeded to abuse[202] the man with foul talk and blasphemy, adding insult to injury: 'Assassin, deserter, you steal what belongs to others and wish to be saved through caring for me. Throw me into the market place[203]—it is meat I crave.'[204] Eulogius brought meat for him.

6. "Again he called out: 'I am not satisfied. Crowds are what I need—I want to go back to the market place! What violence! Take me back where you found me!' Had he had hands to do so, he would quickly have choked Eulogius, so much had the demon exasperated him.

"Eulogius then went off to the ascetics near by and said: 'What should I do? The cripple has led me to despair. Shall I throw him out? I made an oath to God and I fear for myself. But should I not cast him out? I am at a loss to know what to do.'

7. "Then they said: 'As the Great One[205] (for so they called Antony) still lives, go to him. Take the cripple on a boat and bring him to the monastery. Wait until the Great One comes out of his cave and put the case to him. Whatever he tells you, follow his decision, for God speaks to you through him.'

"Now he agreed with them, put the cripple on a rustic bark, and took him to the monastery of Antony's disciples.

8. "Now it happened that the Great Man came the next evening when it was quite late," so Cronius told us, "wrapped in a leather cloak.

"Whenever he came to their monastery, he would call out and ask: 'Brother Macarius, have any brothers come?'

He would answer that they had. 'Are they from Egypt or from Jerusalem?' For he had given him this code for identification: 'If they are easygoing, say that they are Egyptians; if reverend and erudite, say that they are from Jerusalem.'

9. "He asked him then, as was his custom: 'Are they Egyptians, or from Jerusalem?' He answered in reply that it was a mixture.

"Whenever he said they were Egyptians, Antony would say: 'Prepare the lentils and give them to eat.' Then he would say a prayer for them and bid them farewell. But when he said that they were from Jerusalem, then he would sit up all night talking to them about salvation.[206]

10. "On this particular night he seated himself," so he told us, "and he called upon all, and not a single one had told him his name; and when it grew dark he called out: 'Eulogius! Eulogius! Eulogius!'

"Now the aforementioned learned man did not answer, thinking that another Eulogius was being called. Then Antony called again: 'I mean you, Eulogius, you who have come from Alexandria.'

"Eulogius said: 'What do you wish, I beseech you?'

" 'Why did you come?'

"Eulogius replied: 'He who made my name known to you also told you my business.'

11. "Antony said to him: 'I know why you have come, only tell all the brethren, so that they may hear.'

"Eulogius told him: 'I found this cripple in the market place, and I made an oath to God that I would care for him and be saved through him and he through me. Then after all these years he troubles me so that I am of a mind to cast him out. Therefore, I came to Your Holiness so that you may tell me what I should do, and so that you may pray on my behalf, for I am sorely grieved.'

12. "Antony addressed him in a dignified and austere manner: '*You* would cast him out? But *He* who made him does not cast him out. *You* cast him out? God will raise up a finer man than you and He will gather him up.'

"Eulogius kept his peace and cowered. Antony left him and began to lash the cripple verbally and to rail against him:

13. " 'You cripple, maimed, unworthy of either earth or heaven, why do you not stop fighting against God Himself? Do you not realize that it is Christ who is your servant? How dare you utter such things against Christ? Did this man not make himself your servant because of Christ?'

"He was harsh to him, and then he left off. When he had conversed with the rest of them in regard to their wants, he resumed conversation with Eulogius and the cripple in this way:

14. " 'Do not tarry here, but go. Do not separate from each other, except in the cell which you have shared for so long a time. God is even now sending for you. This temptation has come your way as you are both near death and will be judged worthy to be crowned. Therefore, do nothing else, so that the angel may not find you here when he comes.'

"Quickly they made the journey back to their cell. And in forty days Eulogius died, and in three days more the cripple also died."

15. Now Cronius tarried a while[207] about the regions in the Thebaid and then went down to the monasteries of

Alexandria. And it so happened that the brotherhood was observing the forty days for the one and the third day of the other.[208] Cronius learned this and was surprised; he took the Gospel and placed it in the midst of the brethren and told what had happened: "I was the interpreter in these conversations, since the Blessed Antony knew no Greek.[209] I knew both languages and I did the translation, speaking to those two in Greek and to Antony in the Egyptian tongue."[210]

16. Then Cronius told this also:

"On that same night Blessed Antony said: 'For the space of a whole year I used to pray that the place of the just and the sinners be made known to me. And I saw a great giant, high as the clouds, black, with hands outstretched to heaven, and under him a great lake the size of the sea, and I saw souls flying just like birds.[211]

17. " 'And as many as escaped his head and hands were saved, but those that were cuffed by his hands fell into the lake. A great voice came to me saying: "Those are the souls of the just; the souls you see flying into paradise are saved. Those others which are swept into hell are those who followed the desires of the flesh and their own revenge." ' "

22. PAUL THE SIMPLE

1. Cronius and the Blessed Hierax[212] and many others, of whom more later, related in detail the following incident:

"There was a certain Paul,[213] a rustic herdsman, simple and entirely without guile, who was married to a most beautiful woman of debased character. She kept her faults hidden for the longest possible time. When Paul returned from the field without warning, he found them carrying on shamefully.[214] It was Providence which had shown him the way that was best. He smiled and told them: 'Good, all right, it does not matter to me. Jesus help me, I will have nothing more to do with her. Go, have her and her children, too; I am going off to be a monk.'

2. "Telling no one, he hastened away the distance of eight stops[215] and came to the Blessed Antony and knocked at his door.

"Antony came out and asked him: 'What do you want?'

"He said that he wished to become a monk.

"Antony said: 'A man of sixty years, you cannot become a monk here. Go back to your village instead and work, live an active life, giving thanks to God. You would never endure the trials and tribulations of the desert.'

"Again the old man replied: 'I will do whatever you teach me.'

3. "Antony told him: 'I have told you that you are an old man and cannot endure this life. However, if you really wish to become a monk, go to a community of brothers who can put up with your weakness. I live here alone, starving myself with five-day fasts.'

"These are the very arguments he used to scare Paul away. Since he was not going to put up with him, Antony closed the door and did not go out for three days, not even when necessary. But Paul did not go away.

4. "On the fourth day Antony was compelled to go out. He opened the door and told him once more: 'Old man, you must leave this place. Why do you bother me? You cannot remain here.'

"Paul said: 'I cannot die anywhere else but here.'

"Antony observed that he had no food or drink with him, and this was now the fourth day of his fasting. He received him, simply because he feared that the man might die and the guilt would be on his soul. At this time Antony had adopted a way of life more severe than he had ever practiced in his younger days.

5. "So he moistened palm leaves and told him: 'Take these. Weave a rope as I am doing.' The old man wove until the ninth hour, struggling to complete fifteen ells. Antony watched him and was not pleased. 'You wove badly,' he said. 'Unbraid it and begin over.'

"All this distasteful work was imposed on the old man so that he might become irritable and flee from Antony. But he unwove the palm leaves and braided the same ones again, although it was more difficult, because they were wrinkled and dried up. Antony was moved to pity when he noticed that the man did not grumble, or lose heart, or become angry.

6. "When the sun had set, he asked him: 'Are you willing that we eat a piece of bread?'

"Paul replied to this: 'As seems best to you, Father.'

"And again Antony was stabbed to the quick because he did not jump eagerly at the mention of food, but left the decision to the other. He set the table and brought the bread. Antony laid out the biscuits which weighed six ounces and moistened one for himself—for they were dry[216] —and three for him. Then he intoned a psalm which he knew, and when he had sung it twelve times, he prayed twelve times, in order to test Paul.

7. "Paul joined him willingly in prayer again, for he preferred, as I believe, to herd scorpions[217] than to live with an unfaithful wife. After the twelve prayers they

settled down to eat, it being quite late. Antony ate one of
the biscuits, but did not partake of a second. But the old
man was eating his small biscuit slowly, and Antony
waited until he finished and said: 'Eat another one, too,
Father.'

"Paul replied: 'If you eat one, so will I; if you do not,
neither will I.'

"Antony said: 'I have had enough; I am a monk.'

8. " 'I have had enough, too,' said Paul, 'for I wish to
be a monk also.'

"Antony got up then and prayed twelve prayers and
sang twelve psalms. Then he took a little of his first rest,
and at midnight he got up again to sing psalms till it was
day. As he noticed the old man willingly following his
way of life, he said to him: 'If you can do this from day
to day, stay with me.'

"Paul answered: 'If there is anything further, I do not
know, but I can readily do what I have seen.'

"The following day Antony said to him: 'Behold, you
have become a monk.'

9. "When Antony had therefore been fully satisfied
after the specified months[218] that Paul's soul was perfect—
he was very simple and grace cooperated with him—he
built a cell three or four miles away and told him: 'Behold, you have become a monk! Stay here by yourself in
order that you may be tempted by demons.'

"Paul stayed there a year and was deemed worthy of
grace over demons and passions. To cite but one instance:
One most dreadful, possessed as it were by the very
Prince of Demons, one who cursed heaven itself, was
brought to Antony.

10. "Antony looked him over and said to those who

had him: 'This is not my duty, for I have not yet been deemed worthy of power over the ruling order (of demons), but this is Paul's task.'

"Antony left and led them to Paul, to whom he said: 'Father Paul, cast out this demon from the man so that he may return healed to his people.'

"Paul replied: 'What about yourself?'

" 'I have no time,' said Antony, 'I have other work to do.'

"And leaving him, Antony went back to his own cell.

11. "The old man arose, said an efficacious prayer, and addressed the demon-ridden man: 'Father Antony has said that you must leave this man.'

"The demon cursed him roundly and said: 'I am not leaving, you evildoer.'

"Paul took his sheepskin coat and struck him on the back and said: 'Father Antony has told you to go.'

"Then the demon cursed both Antony and Paul still more.

"Finally Paul said: 'You are going to leave or I will go and tell Christ. Jesus help me, if you do not leave, I will go tell Christ now and woe to you what He will do.'

12. "The demon cursed him still more and said: 'I will not leave.'

"Thoroughly enraged at the demon then, Paul went out of his lodging at high noon—now the heat in Egypt is not unlike the Babylonian furnace[219]—and he stood on the rock of the mountain and prayed, saying: 'You see, Jesus Christ, You who were crucified under Pontius Pilate, that I will not come down from the rock, or eat, or drink, until death overtakes me, unless You cast out the spirit from the man and free him.'

13. "Before the words were finished and out of his mouth, the demon cried out and said: 'O violence! I am carried off! The simplicity of Paul drives me out! Where shall I go?'

"And at once the spirit went out and was changed into a great serpent seventy cubits long and was swept into the Red Sea, that the saying might be fulfilled: *The righteous man shall proclaim faith manifest.*[220] This is the marvel of Paul who was called 'the Simple' by the entire brotherhood."

23. PACHON

1. There was a monk named Pachon,[221] about sixty I should judge, who lived in Scete. It so happened that I was troubled by concupiscence both in my thoughts by day and in my dreams at night. My passions were such that I was on the point of leaving the desert, as I had not disclosed this matter to my neighboring monks or to my teacher Evagrius.[222] Without their knowledge I made a trip into the Great Desert and spent fifteen days among the desert fathers at Scete.

2. There I also came across Pachon. As I found him more unworldly and more advanced in the practice of asceticism than the others, I dared to disclose to him my mental condition. And he told me:

"Do not be puzzled at this. You are not suffering because you are easygoing—the place that you are in is of itself witness that you lack necessities and there is no chance of meeting with women—but because of your zealousness. The fight against impurity is threefold: At times concupiscence of the flesh attacks us, and at times the passions work through our thoughts; sometimes the demon himself attacks us in his witchery. I found this out myself by experience.

3. "As you see, I am an old man now. I have been concerned with my salvation for a period of forty years in this very cell—and throughout this time I have been subjected to temptations." And he confirmed this on oath. "For twelve years after my fiftieth year of age the demon relentlessly kept up his attacks, leaving me neither by day nor by night. I suspected that God had abandoned me, and I felt so oppressed that I made up my mind to die in an irrational way rather than give in to bodily passion. I went out then, and while going about the desert, I came across a hyena's cave. Here I placed myself naked one day in hopes that the wild beasts would devour me.

4. "Evening came, and as Sacred Scripture says: *Thou hast appointed darkness, and it is night, in it shall all the beasts of the woods go about.*[223] The beasts, male and female, came out. They smelled me and licked me all over from head to foot. Just when I was expecting to be eaten, they left me. I lay there all night, but they did not devour me.[224] Thinking that God had spared me, I went back to my cell. The demon waited for an opportunity for a few days and then again assailed me even more earnestly than before, so that I was on the verge of blasphemy.

5. "The demon took on the form of an Ethiopian maiden whom I had once seen in my youth gathering papyrus, and sat on my knees.[225] Filled with anger, I gave her a box on the ear and she disappeared. Then for two years I could not bear the evil smell of my hand! Faint of heart and in despair, I went away into the Great Desert. I found a small asp, picked it up, and put it to myself,[226]

so that I might die being bitten in this fashion. Then I ground the head of the reptile into myself[227] as being responsible for my temptation; but I was not bitten.

6. "Then I heard a voice saying in my thoughts: 'Depart, Pachon! Keep up the fight! It was for this reason that I let you be depressed, so that you might not become haughty as a strong person, but rather might know your own weakness, and that you might not trust too much in your own way of life, but rather come running to God for help.'

"I returned then fully satisfied, and I settled down confidently, worrying no more about the struggle, but dwelling in peace the rest of my days. The demon who knew my contempt for him no longer came near."

24. STEPHEN

1. Stephen,[228] a Libyan by nationality, resided on the Marmarican[229] and Mareotic[230] coast for some sixty years. He had attained the highest degree of asceticism, and he was accounted worthy of discernment of grace.[231] Every one who came to him suffering any kind of affliction went away cured. He was also an acquaintance of the Blessed Antony, and he lived down to our own time. I never met him, however, because he was so far off.

2. But those around Saints Ammonius and Evagrius told me this: "We found on arrival that he had fallen prey to the terrible ulcerous condition known as cancer.[232] We found him under the care of a physician. He was working with his hands and weaving palm leaves and he conversed with us while his body was undergoing an operation. He acted as though it were someone else who was undergoing

the knife. While his members were being cut away like locks of hair, he showed no sign whatsoever of pain, thanks to the superiority of his spiritual preparation.

3. "While we were grieving at this and were appalled that a person who lived a life like his should suffer disease and such surgical remedies, he told us: 'My children, do not be hurt by this. Of all the things God does, not one is done out of evil intent, but all are for a good purpose. It may well be that my members deserve punishment and it would be better to pay the penalty here than after I have left the arena.'[233] Thus he encouraged and edified us with his exhortations."

Now I have told this so that we may not be puzzled when we see holy people falling prey to sickness.

25. VALENS

1. There was one named Valens,[234] by nationality a Palestinian, but by disposition a Corinthian—for Saint Paul charged the Corinthians with arrogance.[235] He took to the desert and lived among us for several years. Then he reached such a state of arrogance that demons attacked him. From deceiving him a little they went so far as to make him believe he was in league with the angels.

2. One day, so the story goes at any rate, he was working in the dark and lost the needle with which he was stitching up a basket. When he could not find the needle, a demon produced a lamp and he found it. Another time he became very conceited, so much so that he felt he was too good to partake of the Mysteries. Then it so happened that some guests brought pastries to the church for the brethren.

3. The holy Macarius,[236] our superior, took them and sent about a handful apiece to each of us in our cells, and to Valens as well. Then Valens, seizing and striking the one who carried them, cursed him, saying: "Go, tell Macarius that I am no worse than you that he should send me a gift."[237]

Now Macarius knew that he was far off, and he went the next day to talk to him. He said to him: "Valens, you were deceived![238] Stop at once!"

As Valens did not listen to his exhortations, he went away.

4. The demon then was fully satisfied that Valens was completely won over by his treachery, and he went and disguised himself as the Saviour. He appeared at night in a vision of a thousand angels carrying lamps and a fiery disc in which, so it seemed to Valens, the Saviour had taken shape, and an angel approached Valens, saying: "Christ has loved you because of your way of life and your liberality to Him, and He has come to visit you. Leave your cell now, and you have only to retire to some distance to behold Him, kneel down to do homage to Him, and then go back to your cell."

5. So he went out, and when he saw marshalled in line those who carried lamps, and the Antichrist himself about a stade or so away, he fell down and adored. The next day he became so obsessed again that he went into the church and told all the assembled brethren: "I have no use for Communion, for I saw Christ this very day."

Then the fathers bound him and put him in irons for a year. They changed him through their prayers and the living of an ordinary, unbusied life. As the saying goes: "Diseases are cured by their opposites."[239]

6. It is useful to insert in this little volume the lives of such as these (just as among the holy trees of Paradise there was the tree that gives knowledge of good and evil)[240] as a caution for those who come across it, so that if they ever do a good act, they might not become too puffed up in their virtues. Often, indeed, even a virtue, whenever it is not perfected with the right intention, may be responsible for a fall. For it is written: *I saw a just man perishing in his justice, and this thing is indeed vanity*.[241]

26. HERON

1. One of my neighbors, Heron,[242] by nationality an Alexandrian, a courteous and good-natured young man who led a pure life, was thrown off balance after many labors and exalted himself, feeling himself greater than the fathers. He even insulted the blessed Evagrius, saying: "Those who obey your teaching are deceived. One need not pay attention to any teachers but Christ." He even misused Scripture to serve his foolish purpose and said: "The Saviour Himself said: *Call no one teacher upon the earth*."[243]

2. Then he became so blind in his folly that later he, too, was put into irons when he refused to partake of the Mysteries—dear is truth.[244] He was extremely sparing in his way of life, as many say he used to partake of food only every three months, being satisfied with the Communion of the Mysteries and a little wild lettuce if some should come his way. I had an experience with him myself traveling with the blessed Albanius[245] to Scete.

3. Now Scete was forty miles away from us, and in that distance we partook of food twice and drank water

three times, but he went along on foot without taking a thing. He recited by heart fifteen psalms, then the long psalm,[246] then the Epistle to the Hebrews, then Isaias and a portion of Jeremias, then Luke the Evangelist, and finally Proverbs. As it was we could not keep step with him as he hurried along.

4. Finally he was driven as though it were by fire, and he could not remain in his cell. So he went off to Alexandria by a special dispensation, so he called it, and drove out a nail with a nail.[247] He fell wilfully into a dissolute life and later found salvation against his will. He went to the theatre and the horse races and haunted the taverns. Eating and drinking to excess, he fell into the filth of lust. And since he was bent upon committing sin,[248] he met an actress and had commerce with her. This led to an ulcer. While this affair was going on, a carbuncle developed on him,[249] and for half a year he was so ill that his members became infested with rot and fell off. Subsequently he was restored to health without these members[250] and he came back to a pious resolution and confessed everything to the fathers.[251] Some days later he fell asleep[252] just before going to work.[253]

27. PTOLEMY

1. Again, there was another monk, one named Ptolemy,[254] who lived a life hard to describe, or rather, I should say, impossible of description. He lived out beyond Scete in a place called "The Ladder,"[255] an uninhabitable place, as the brothers' well is eighteen miles away. He used to come there bringing along a good many Cilician pots,[256] and during the months of December and January he used

to collect the dew from the rocks with a sponge, for there was a goodly amount of dew there. The fifteen years he lived there, the water sufficed for him.

2. He became estranged from the teaching and company of holy men and their help and the continual Communion of the Mysteries.[257] He reached such a pitch of nonsense as to say that these things are nothing. Report has it that he is borne about Egypt suspended aloft in his pride and has given himself over to gluttony and wine-bibbing, setting no good example to anyone. Now this Ptolemy suffered misfortune because of his illogical thinking; as Holy Writ has it: *Where there is no governor the people shall fall like leaves.*[258]

28. THE VIRGIN FALLEN FROM GRACE

I knew a maiden in Jerusalem who wore sackcloth[259] for six years and was immured, partaking of none of the things which pertain to pleasure. Finally she fell completely abandoned because of her overweening pride. She opened her door and received the man who had ministered to her, and she committed sin with him, because she had practiced asceticism for the sake of human applause[260] rather than for religious purposes and out of the love of God. Vainglory and evil intentions are the cause of that. For as her thoughts were occupied in running down others, the guardian of her chastity was absent.[261]

29. ELIAS

1. A certain ascetic, Elias,[262] had great concern for the virgins; for there are souls like that whose virtuous

purpose testifies for them. He showed compassion on the order of women ascetics and, as he had income-property in Athribé,[263] he built a large monastery and gathered together all those dispersed about into this monastery. He looked after them, providing them with every refreshment, gardens, household utensils, and everything their life required. These women, gathered from every walk of life, quarrelled continuously with each other.

2. Since he had to listen to their arguments and act as peacemaker—for he had gathered together about three hundred of them—it was necessary for him to stay in their midst for a two-year period. Being still young, between thirty and forty years of age, he was tempted by lust. He went away from the monastery and fasted for two days. This was his prayer: "O Lord, either kill me outright, so that I may not have to see these women wrangling, or take away my passion, so that I may look after them in a reasonable way."

3. When evening came he slept out in the desert. Three angels came to him, as he used to say, and they seized him and said: "Why did you leave the women's monastery?"

He explained the circumstances to them: "Because I was afraid that I might bring harm to them and to myself as well."

"Now if we take away your passion," they asked, "will you go back and look after them?"

He gave his assent to this and they exacted an oath from him.

4. He said that this was the oath: "Swear to us: 'By Him who looks after me, I will look after them.' "

And he swore to them. They took hold of him, one by the hands and one by the feet, and the third took a razor and castrated him—not actually, but in the dream.[264] Then it seemed to him, in this vision, as one might say, that he was cured.

They asked him: "Do you notice the advantage?"

"I feel greatly relieved," he said, "and I really believe that I am cured of my passion."

5. They told him to leave then. He went back after five days and the whole community was mourning for him. He entered and remained indoors from that time in a near-by cell from which he gave advice as best he could, being close enough at hand. But he lived forty years longer and told the fathers: "Passion comes no more to my mind."

Such was the grace of that saint who looked out for the monastery in that way.

30. DOROTHEUS

Dorotheus[265] was his successor, a most excellent man who had grown old in a praiseworthy active life. Since he could not stay in the monastery itself, he closed himself in an upper story and made a window overlooking the women's part of the monastery. He could shut and open this window where he sat, constantly exhorting[266] the women not to fight. He grew old in the upper story. No women came up to him, and he did not go down to them, for there was no ladder placed there.

31. PIAMOUN

1. Piamoun[267] was a virgin who lived with her mother spinning flax and eating only every other day at evening.

She was deemed worthy of the gift of prophecy, a case in point being the time the river overflowed in Egypt and one village attacked another. They were fighting about the water distribution[268] and this resulted in blows and even murder. A more powerful town attacked her village, and a crowd of men was coming with spears and cudgels to devastate her village.

2. An angel appeared to her and revealed their attack. So she sent for the elders of the village and said to them: "Go out and talk with those who are coming here from that village, lest you all die along with the populace, and tell them to put an end to their hatred."

Now the elders were afraid, and they fell at her feet, begging her, and said: "We cannot come to an agreement with them, for we know their drunkenness and frenzy. But if you have mercy on the whole town and your own home, go out and make peace with them yourself."

She did not agree to this, but she did go to her own abode and she stood all night praying, never bending her knees. She besought the Lord, praying: "Lord, who judges the world, whom nothing unjust pleases, now when this prayer reaches You, may Your power fix them to the place wherever it may find them."

4. And along about the first hour, when they were about three miles away, they were fixed to the spot and could not budge. It was made known to them that this hindrance was due to her intercession. So they sent to the village, suing for peace, making it clear that this was "because of God and the prayers of Piamoun, for they stopped us."

32. PACHOMIUS AND THE TABENNESIOTES[269]

1. The so-called Tabennisi[270] is a place in the Thebaid where lived a certain Pachomius,[271] a man of the kind who live rightly, so that he was deemed worthy of prophecies and angelic visions. He became exceedingly kind and brotherly. One time when he was sitting in his cave an angel appeared to him and told him: "So far as you are concerned, you conduct your life perfectly. It is vain for you to continue sitting in your cave! Come now, leave this place and go out and call the young monks together and dwell with them. Rule them by the model which I am now giving you."

And the angel gave him a bronze tablet[272] on which this was engraved:

2. "You will let each one eat and drink as suits his strength; and divide up their tasks in accord with their respective strengths, and not hinder anyone from fasting or eating. Assign the more difficult tasks to the stronger ones who eat, and assign lesser tasks to those who are weak and more ascetic. Make separate cells in the cloister and let there be three monks to a cell. Meals, however, should be taken by all in one house.

3. "Let them not recline at full length, but let them take their rest sitting down on their coverlets thrown over the backs of chairs. At night they may wear lebitons.[273] Let each one have a coat of worked goatskin; they may not eat without it. On Saturday and Sunday when they go to Communion, they may loosen their girdles and go in with the hood only."

He fashioned cowls for them which were without hair,

as a child's, and he ordered a brand in the form of a cross
to be added in purple.

4. He arranged them in twenty-four groups, and to
each group he assigned a letter of the Greek alphabet,[274]
beginning with alpha, beta, gamma, delta, and so on.
When he asked questions or carried on the community
business he would ask the prefect: "How is the Alpha section? How is Zeta doing?" Or again: "Give greetings to
Rho."

They followed a special meaning which was given to
the letters. "To the simpler and less worldly you shall assign the iota; but to the more difficult and headstrong, the
chi."

5. And so he fitted the letters to each order according
to their state of life and disposition; but only the more
spiritual ones knew the meaning of each symbol.

On the tablet was engraved: "A strange monk of another monastery[275] may not eat or drink or stay with them
unless he is really on a journey. And one who has come to
stay they do not receive into the sanctuary[276] for a period
of three years. When such a one has performed the more
laborious works, however, he is received, but only after a
three-year period.

6. "When they are eating, let them cover their heads
with their cowls, so that a brother may not perceive his
neighbor chewing. Nor should one talk while eating or
cast his eye from his own plate or table."[277]

He commanded that they pray twelve prayers each day
and twelve at lamp-lighting time, and that at all-night de-
votions they say twelve prayers, and three at the ninth
hour.[278] When the group was about to eat, he commanded
them to sing a psalm in addition to each prayer.[279]

7. When Pachomius objected to the angel that the prayers were too few, the angel said: "I arranged it this way so that even the little ones[280] might keep the rule and not grieve. Now those who are perfect need no rule of life, for they have offered themselves entirely to the contemplation of God in their cells. I have made rules for such as have not the true knowledge,[281] so that they may fulfill the duties of their station in life like house-servants and so enjoy a life of complete liberty."[282]

8. There were some monasteries which abided by this rule and they totaled seven thousand men. First of all there was the great monastery where Pachomius himself lived. This is the mother of all the other monasteries, having thirteen hundred men,[283] among whom was Aphthonius the Good,[284] well known to me as a friend, who is now second monk in the monastery. They used to send him to Alexandria to sell produce and buy the necessities, as he is the least apt to go astray.

9. There are other monasteries, too, housing from two to three hundred persons each. I visited one of these when I went to Panapolis,[285] a place of about three hundred monks. In this monastery I saw fifteen tailors, seven workers in metal, four carpenters, twelve camel drivers, and fifteen fullers. They work at every sort of handicraft and from their surplus they provide for the monasteries of women and the prison.

10. They even keep swine. When I objected to that practice, they answered me: "With us it is an old custom that they are nourished with the refuse and vegetable leftovers. What is dropped is thrown out, and in this way is saved. The pigs are killed and their flesh is sold, but the pigs' feet are given to the sick and the old, as the territory

is poor but heavily populated, for the tribe of the Blem-myes[286] also lives close by."

11. Now those appointed to serve for the day rise early and go to the kitchen or to the refectory. They are employed until mealtime in preparing and setting the tables, putting on each table loaves of bread, charlock, preserved olives, cheese made of cow's milk, and small vegetables. Some come in and eat at the sixth hour, others at the seventh, others at the eighth, others at the ninth, others at the eleventh, still others at late evening, some every other day, so that each group knows its own proper hour.

12. It is the same with regard to their work. One works the ground as husbandman, another works as gardener, another as smith, another as baker, another as fuller, another as weaver of large baskets, another as shoemaker, another as copyist, another as weaver of tender reeds. They all learn the Holy Scriptures by heart.[287]

33. THE WOMEN'S MONASTERY

1. In addition to these there was also a monastery of some four hundred women. They had the same sort of management and the same way of life,[288] except for the cloak. The women lived on one side of the river opposite the men. When a virgin died, the others laid her out for burial, and they carried her body and placed it on the bank of the river. The brethren would cross on a ferry-boat and carrying palm leaves and olive branches bring the body over and bury it in the common cemetery.

2. No one goes over to the women's monastery except the priest and deacon, and they go only on Sunday.

This incident took place in that monastery: A tailor of

the world crossed over through ignorance, looking for work. A young virgin came out—the place was deserted—and heard his story. She answered him: "We have our own tailors."

3. Another virgin saw this happen, and a while later, when an argument ensued, she was stirred up by a diabolical motive and her mind was so deranged that she made a false accusation against the other to the rest of the sisterhood. A few others joined her in this wicked act. The other was so grieved at undergoing this persecution, since she had not had the slightest idea of committing such a sin, that she could remain there no longer and she secretly threw herself into the river and died.

4. The talebearer, realizing the guilt on her own part in her false accusation, aware that she was the one who had brought about the crime, could stand it no longer and hanged herself.

The other sisters told the whole story to the priest when he came. He ordered that the Sacrifice was not to be offered for either of them. As for those who did not effect a reconciliation when they knew the charge was completely false and still were willing to believe their story, he separated them from the others and forbade them to receive Communion for a period of seven years.[289]

34. THE NUN WHO FEIGNED MADNESS

1. In this monastery there was another maiden who feigned madness and demon-possession. The others felt such contempt for her that they never ate with her, which pleased her entirely. Taking herself to the kitchen she used to perform every menial service[290] and she was, as the

saying goes, "the sponge of the monastery,"[291] really ful-
filling the Scriptures: *If any man among you seem to be
wise in this world, let him become a fool that he may be
wise.*[292] She wore a rag around her head—all the others had
their hair closely cropped and wore cowls. In this way she
used to serve.

2. Not one of the four hundred ever saw her chewing
all the years of her life. She never sat down at table or partook of a particle of bread, but she wiped up with a sponge
the crumbs from the tables and was satisfied with scouring
pots. She was never angry at anyone, nor did she grumble
or talk, either little or much, although she was maltreated,
insulted, cursed, and loathed.

3. Now an angel appeared to Saint Piteroum,[293] the
famous anchorite dwelling at Porphyrites,[294] and said to
him: "Why do you think so much of yourself for being
pious and residing in a place such as this? Do you want to
see someone more pious than yourself, a woman? Go to
the women's monastery at Tabennisi and there you will
find one with a band on her head. She is better than you
are.

4. "While being cuffed about by such a crowd she has
never taken her heart off God. But you dwell here and
wander about cities in your mind."

And he who had never gone away left that monastery
and asked the prefects to allow him to enter into the monastery of women. They admitted him, since he was well
on in years and, moreover, had a great reputation.

5. So he went in and insisted upon seeing all of them.
She did not appear. Finally he said to them: "Bring them
all to me, for she is missing."

They told him: "We have one inside in the kitchen

who is touched"²⁹⁵—that is what they call the afflicted ones.

He told them: "Bring her to me. Let me see her."

They went to call her; but she did not answer, either because she knew of the incident or because it was revealed to her. They seized her forcibly and told her: "The holy Piteroum wishes to see you"—for he was renowned.

6. When she came he saw the rag on her head and, falling down at her feet, he said: "Bless me!"

In similar manner she too fell down at his feet and said: "Bless me, lord."

All the women were amazed at this and said: "Father, take no insults. She is touched."

Piteroum then addressed all the women: "You are the ones who are touched! This woman is spiritual mother"²⁹⁶ —so they called them spiritually—"to both you and me and I pray that I may be deemed as worthy as she on the Day of Judgment."

7. Hearing this, they fell at his feet, confessing various things—one how she had poured the leavings of her plate over her; another had beaten her with her fists; another had blistered her nose. So they confessed various and sundry outrages. After praying for them, he left. And after a few days she was unable to bear the praise and honor of the sisters, and all their apologizing was so burdensome to her that she left the monastery. Where she went and where she disappeared to, and how she died, nobody knows.

35. JOHN OF LYCOPOLIS

1. It happened there was one John²⁹⁷ of Lycopolis²⁹⁸ who learned the building trade as a boy. His father was a

dyer. Later, when he was about twenty-five, he left the world. After he had lived in various monasteries for five years, he went off alone to the mountain of Lyco. There, on the very top of the mountain, he built himself three cells,[299] went inside, and housed himself there. One cell was for his bodily needs; he worked and ate in the second; in the third one he prayed.

2. After he had completed thirty years in confinement, receiving the necessities of life from one who waited on him through a window, he was deemed worthy of the gift of prophecy.[300] Among other things he dispatched various predictions to the blessed Emperor Theodosius in regard to Maximus the tyrant, that he would conquer him and return from the Gauls.[301] Likewise he brought him the glad tidings about the tyrant Eugenius.[302] So his fame as a virtuous man spread.

3. While we were in the Nitrian Desert, I and those who were in the company of the blessed Evagrius, we sought to find out precisely what the virtue of that man was. The blessed Evagrius said: "Gladly would I learn what kind of a man he is from the testimony of one who knows how to interpret mind and speech. Since I myself cannot see him, I could hear exactly from another man of his way of life, but I shall not go so far as the mountain."

I heard him and I did not tell a soul, but rather kept silence all day. The following day I locked up my cell, and entrusting it and myself to God, I made off for the Thebaid.

4. And I got there after eighteen days, partly on foot, partly by sailing along the river. It was the time of the inundation of the Nile when many take sick, and I, too, fell a victim. When I arrived, I found his vestibule locked

(later on the brothers enlarged the vestibule considerably, so that it holds about a hundred men); they had locked it up, but opened it on Saturday and Sunday. When I learned the reason, therefore, for its being closed, I kept my peace until Saturday. I came at the second hour to meet him and I found him sitting at the window where he would appear to console those who happened to be there.

5. He greeted me then and spoke through an interpreter.[303] "Where are you from and why did you come? I presume that you are from Evagrius' company?"

I told him: "I am a stranger come from Galatia."

I also admitted that I belonged to the group of Evagrius. And as we talked Alypius,[304] the governor of the place, approached. He joined Alypius and broke off speaking to me. I withdrew a little and yielded space to them, standing a little way off. They kept on conversing for quite a while. I grew tired and exhausted and I murmured against the old man for spurning me and giving the other the place of honor.

6. Disgusted at this, I intended simply to ignore him and leave. He summoned his interpreter Theodore and told him: "Go, tell that brother: 'Do not be petty; right now I am about to send the governor away and I will speak to you.'"

So it seemed best to me to wait patiently and regard him as a spiritual man. And when the governor had gone he called to me and said: "Why are you angry with me? What do you find so blameworthy that you would think such things which are neither true of me nor proper for you? Or do you not know that it is written: *They that are whole need not the physician, but they that are sick?*[305] I find you when I want you and you find me.

7. "And if I do not give consolation to you, there are other brothers and fathers to give you consolation. That man was delivered to the devil because of his worldly deeds, and he enjoyed a short breathing spell just like a servant who has run away from his master. He came to be helped. It would be out of place to abandon him in order to spend the time with you as long as you are always free to take care of your own salvation."

I asked him to pray for me, being fully aware that he was a spiritual man.

8. So then he playfully struck my left cheek with his right hand and told me: "Many sorrows await you, and many things have worked against you to get you to leave the desert. You were terrified and put off your resolution. The demon brings up pious and well-sounding excuses for you and weakens you. He suggested to you a desire to see your father and to instruct your brother and sister in the solitary life.

9. "Now look, I have good news for you. Both are saved, for they have been converted.[306] And your father still has many more years ahead of him. Therefore, persevere in the desert and do not wish to leave for your country on their account, for it is written: *No man putting his hand to the plow and looking back is fit for the Kingdom of God.*"[307]

I was helped by these words, and I gave thanks to God when I found that the excuses that were tormenting me were destroyed.

10. Then he spoke to me jokingly: "Do you wish to be a bishop?"

I said: "I already am."

And he: "Where?"

I said: "In the kitchen and shops, over the tables and pots. I examine[308] them, and if there is any sour wine I excommunicate it, but I drink the good. Likewise I inspect the pots, too, and if any salt or other spices are lacking, I throw these in and thus season them and eat them. This is my diocese, for Gluttony has ordained me for her child."

11. He said smiling: "Stop playing with words. As bishop you would have to be ordained and labor much and suffer many tribulations. If indeed you would flee the tribulations, you would not leave the desert. No one has the power to ordain you bishop here in the desert."

I left him then, went back to my own accustomed place in the desert, and told everything to the blessed fathers. They sailed away two months later and met him. I forgot his advice, but after three years I fell sick with an ailment of the spleen and stomach.

12. From there I was sent to Alexandria by the brotherhood to be cured of hydropsy. The physicians advised me to go from Alexandria to Palestine on account of the climate, for there the air is lighter[309] for our constitution. From Palestine I went to Bithynia and there—whether because of human eagerness or because of the good will of Him who is more powerful, I do not now know; God would know[310]—I was thought worthy of ordination since I had taken part in the state of affairs connected with the blessed John.[311]

13. And so for eleven months I was hidden away in a dark cell,[312] and I remembered that blessed man and suffered everything he had foretold.

This he had told me as a help for enduring the desert: "Forty years have I been in this cell, never beholding a woman's face or the sight of money. I have seen no one eating, nor has anyone seen me eating or drinking."

14. He did not entertain Poimenia,[313] the servant of God, when she came to visit him, but he cleared up for her a number of secret things. He told her not to turn aside to Alexandria on her way down from the Thebaid, "for there you must fall into temptation." Now she either deceived him outright or else forgot about that advice. She did turn aside to Alexandria to see the city for herself. On the journey she had her boats tied up near Nicopolis[314] to wait for her.

15. When her servants went ashore they had a fight with the natives, very desperate men, because of some kind of disorder. Some cut off the finger of a eunuch; another one they killed; not recognizing the saintly bishop Dionysius, they doused him in the river. After they had wounded all the other servants, they insulted and threatened her.

36. POSIDONIUS

1. Stories told about Posidonius[315] the Theban are hard to relate and are very many indeed—how great his meekness was, and what a great ascetic he was, and how complete was his goodness. I do not think I ever met another such as he was. For I lived with him for a year in Bethlehem when he lived beyond Poimenion,[316] and I was witness to his many virtues.

2. One day he told me this, among his other stories: "I dwelt in the place called Porphyrites[317] for the space of a year in which I met no man, heard no conversation, and touched no bread; but I managed with a few dates from time to time and any sort of wild herbs which I found.

Then when food was entirely lacking, I left the cave to go back to civilization.

3. "So I walked all day and I got scarcely two miles from the cave. Then I looked about and saw a charioteer who looked like a soldier with a tiara-like helmet on his head. I thought he was a soldier, so I hurried back to the cave—and I found a basket of grapes and newly cut figs. I took up the basket and entered the cave, very grateful for such food, a consolation after two months of starving."

4. This is the wonder he performed in Bethlehem: There was a pregnant woman who had an unclean spirit, and she was in great travail when she was about to give birth, for the spirit was bothering her. As she was possessed by the evil spirit, her husband got up and came to ask the holy man to come. When we came in together to pray, he stood up, and the second time he knelt down he drove out the spirit.[318]

5. He arose and spoke to us: "Pray, for the unclean spirit is even now leaving; there has to be a sign in order for us to be fully assured."

So the demon when he left knocked down the wall of the hall from its foundations. The woman had not spoken for a period of six years, but after the spirit went out of her she bore the child and spoke.

6. I knew of this prophecy made by this man: A priest, Jerome,[319] dwelt in the same place; he was a man of good birth and well gifted in Latin letters, but he had such a disposition[320] that it eclipsed his learning. Posidonius had lived with him a goodly number of days and he whispered into my ear: "The fine Paula[321] who takes care of him is going to die and escape his meanness, I believe.

7. "And because of him no holy man will live in these

parts. His anger would drive out even his own brother."

And so it happened, for he drove out the blessed Oxy-perentius, the Italian, and another holy man, Peter the Egyptian,[322] and Simeon,[323] wonderful men on whom I then put my mark of approval.

Posidonius told me that he did not try bread for forty years, nor did he hold a grudge against anyone for even half a day.

37. SARAPION

1. There was another, Sarapion, nicknamed Sindo-nites,[324] for he never wore anything but a loincloth. He practiced the greatest poverty and was highly literate;[325] that accounts for his knowing the Sacred Scriptures by heart. Even with this great poverty and meditation upon the Scriptures he could not remain quiet in his cell. It was not that he was distracted by material things; he wandered about the world and successfully perfected this virtue, for that was his nature. For there are differences in natures, but not in substances.[326]

2. The fathers used to tell how he took an ascetic for a companion and sold himself to some Greek[327] actors in one of the towns for twenty coins. He wrapped up the coins and kept them on himself. He stayed with the actors who had bought him for a long time, until he had made them Christians, and then withdrew from the theatre, tak-ing nothing but bread and water. Nor did his mouth ever cease from discussing the Scriptures.

3. After some time the actor was seized with compas-sion, then the actress, then their whole family. It was said that for as long as they did not recognize him, he would

even wash the feet of both of them. In any case, both were baptized and gave up performing on the stage. They led a holy and pious life, and they had the highest respect for him and told him: "Come, brother, let us set you free, since you freed us from our shameful slavery."

He said to them: "Since God worked grace in your souls and saved you, I may tell you the secrets of my business.

4. "I had compassion on your souls. I am a free man, and an Egyptian ascetic, and I sold myself for your sakes so that you might be saved. Now since God brought this about and your souls have been saved through my debasement, take your money so that I may go and help others."

They entreated him and gave their assurance that "we will have you as our own father and master—only stay with us!" Still they could not persuade him. Then they told him: "Give the money to the poor, for it is our first pledge for salvation.[328] But at least visit us once a year."

5. In his continual journeys he arrived at Greece and stayed three days at Athens, and now no one gave him bread. No, he did not carry any money, or purse or cloak, or any such. As the fourth day came on he was exceedingly hungry—for hunger, if it is not voluntary, is terrible, especially if it is accompanied by misbelief. So he stood up on a high place on a hill in the city and began to lament bitterly, clapping his hands and calling out: "Help, O men of Athens!"

6. And they all came running up to him, philosophers and laborers alike,[329] saying: "What ails you? Where are you from? What is the matter with you?"

He said: "As for race, I am from Egypt. When I left my own country, I fell into the hands of three moneylenders. Two of them were fully satisfied when they left me; they had no further claims to make. But one of them has not left me."

Now they busied themselves about the creditors so that they might satisfy themselves and they asked him: "Where are they? And who are they? Who is it that bothers you? Show us that we may help you."

7. Then he told them: "From my youth covetousness and greed and unchastity plagued me. I am free of two of these, namely covetousness and unchastity; they no longer torment me. But I cannot shake off greed. For four days now I have not eaten, and my stomach persists in grumbling, accustomed as it is to daily fare, without which I cannot live."

Then some of the philosophers, supposing that he was acting a part, gave him a coin. This he took and spent in a baker's shop for a loaf of bread, and he immediately took to the road and never came back there again.

8. Then the philosophers knew how truly virtuous he was. They gave the baker the price of the bread and took back the coin which he had paid.[330]

He went on to Lacedemonia and heard about one of the first men of the city who together with his whole family was Manichaean, but righteous in everything else. He sold himself to this man as in the earlier case, and within two years he had turned the man and his wife away from heresy to the Church. Then they no longer regarded him as a servant, but as a relative, a brother, or a father, and they gave glory to God.

9. He boarded a vessel with the intention of sailing to Rome. The sailors supposed either that he had paid the price of the journey or that he had the fare; they accepted

him as a passenger in a casual manner, each one thinking he had paid the other. When they had set sail and were five hundred stades from Alexandria, the travelers began to eat around sunset, as the crew had eaten earlier.

10. Then they saw that he did not eat the first day, and they supposed it was because of the sailing.[330a] Likewise the second, the third, and the fourth day. On the fifth day they observed him sitting quietly while the others were eating and they asked him: "Man, why do you not eat?"

He said: "Because I have nothing."

Thereupon they asked among themselves: "Who took his fare or his money?"

11. And when they found that no one had, they began to belabor him and say: "How can you come without money for travel? Where will you get the fare for us? And what do you have to eat?"

He told them: "I have nothing. Take me back and throw me out where you found me!"

Now they would not have given up their trip for a hundred gold pieces, so they kept on their course. Thus it was that he was on the ship and they found themselves feeding him until they got to Rome.

12. Upon arriving at Rome he inquired whether there were any great ascetics, either male or female, in the city. He happened to meet one Domninus,[331] a disciple of Origen whose bed cured sick persons after his death. He met him and was helped by him, for he was a well-rounded man, of good birth and educated. He learned from him of ascetics, both men and women, and of a maiden living in seclusion who did not meet anyone.[332]

13. Upon finding where she lived he departed and said

to the old woman who looked after her: "Tell the maiden that it is most necessary that I meet her, for God has sent me." After waiting two or three days, he met her and asked her: "Why do you keep sitting?"

She said: "I do not sit, but I travel."

He said: "Where do you travel?"

And she: "To God."

He asked her: "Are you living or dead?"

She answered: "I believe in God that I am dead, for no one in the flesh makes that journey."

He said: "So that you may indeed convince me you are dead, do what I do."

She told him: "Command what is possible and I will do it."

14. He replied to her: "Everything is possible to a dead person, except to commit an act of impiety." Then he told her: "Go out and show yourself."

She answered him: "For twenty-five years I have been here and not gone out. Why should I go out?"

He told her: "If you are dead to the world and the world to you,[333] it is the same to you whether you go out or not. Therefore, go out."

She went out then, and after she had appeared in public and gone to some church, he spoke to her there: "Now, if you wish really to convince me you are dead and no longer alive, pleasing men,[334] do as I do and I will know that you are dead.

15. "Disrobe yourself and place your clothing on your shoulders and go through the middle of the city with me in the lead in this way."[335]

She said to him: "I would scandalize many doing such

an indecent thing and they would have to say: 'That one is insane and demon-ridden.'"

He told her: "And so far as you are concerned, what does it matter that they say you are insane and demon-ridden?"

Then she told him: "If you wish anything else, I will do it; for I do not boast that I have come to this point."

16. Then he told her: "See now, do not consider yourself more pious than the others, or dead to the world, for I am more dead in that sense than you are; in fact I will show you that I am dead to the world, for I will do this without shame and without feeling." Thus he left her humbled and broke her pride.

There are many other wonders which he did also proving his perfect self-control. He died at the age of sixty, and he is buried in Rome itself.[336]

38. EVAGRIUS

1. It would not be right to pass over in silence the famous deacon Evagrius,[337] a man who lived in truly apostolic fashion. One should put these things in writing for the spiritual edification of those who happen to come across this account and for the glory of the goodness of our Saviour. I believe it worthwhile to set forth from the beginning, to tell how he arrived at his goal and how he practiced asceticism in the right way and then died in the desert at the age of fifty-four. As Scripture has it, *in a short time he fulfilled many years.*[338]

2. He was of the Pontic race, of the city of Ibora,[339] son of a chorbishop,[340] and he was ordained lector by Saint

Basil, bishop of the church at Caesarea.[341] Then after the death of Saint Basil,[342] the bishop Gregory of Nazianzus, a man most wise, most serene, and brilliant in learning, took note of his fitness and ordained him deacon.[343] Then in the great synod at Constantinople he left him to the blessed bishop Nectarius[344] as one most skillful in confuting all the heresies. He flourished in the great city, confuting every heresy with youthful exuberance.

3. Now it so happened that he, honored as he was by the entire city, was ensnared in the contemplation of desire for a woman, as he later told us when he was freed of the thought. This woman also loved him in return. She was of the highest social class. So Evagrius, with a fear of God and a respect for his own conscience, perceived plainly the magnitude of the disgrace and the delight which heretics would take in his transgression, and he prayed humbly to God to put some impediment in his path. He wished to break off with the woman, who by now was eager and frantic, but he could not do so, so caught up was he in the bonds of concupiscence.

4. After he had been at prayer a short time, there appeared to him an angelic vision[345] in which soldiers of the governor took him and led him into custody as it were, having bound him with iron collars, put chains on his neck, and tied his hands. They did not tell him why. But he knew in his own conscience that this was because of what he had done, and he thought that the woman's husband had brought this about.

5. And now he was very much worried, for another trial was going on with others being tried for some complaint or other. The angel who had brought the vision changed its form as it were into that of a genuine friend

and spoke to him while he was then roped together with forty criminals: "Why is His Deaconship detained here?"

"To be sure, I do not know, but I suspect that the governor has a charge against me and is smitten by some silly jealousy, and I am afraid that the judge himself will be bribed with money and may punish me."

6. The angel said: "Listen to a friend. It will not be safe for you to stay on in this town."

Evagrius told him: "Let God free me from this predicament, and if you still see me in Constantinople, know that I would undergo this punishment without complaint."

Then the vision spoke: "I will bring the Gospel; you swear on it that you will leave this town and will have concern for your soul, and I will free you from this strait."

7. The Gospel was brought then and he swore to him by it: "Except for this one day when I am packing to leave, I shall not tarry here longer."

As the oath was finished he came back out of his ecstasy. He got up and decided that "even if this oath was made in my vision, nevertheless I did swear it." Putting everything aboard ship, he went on to Jerusalem.

8. And there he was greeted by that Roman lady, the blessed Melania. Soon the devil hardened his heart, as in the case of Pharaoh.[346] And as he was young and filled with uncertainty and in a dilemma, he mentioned nothing to anyone and returned to his old life, changing his clothes and his manner of speech—he was intoxicated with vainglory. But the One who hinders destruction for us all, God Himself, checked him by bringing a six-month fever upon him. This wasted away his flesh which had been his great impediment.

9. Now when the doctors were in a quandary and

could find no treatment to cure him, the blessed Melania addressed him: "Son, I am not pleased with your long sickness. Tell me what is in your mind, for your sickness is not beyond God's aid."

Then he confessed the whole story.

She told him: "Promise me by the Lord that you mean to aim at the monastic life, and even though I am a sinner, I will pray that you be given a lease on life."

He agreed, and was well again in a matter of days. He got up, received a change of clothing at her hands,[347] then left and took himself to the mountain of Nitria in Egypt.

10. He lived there for two years, and in the third year he went off to the desert. Then he lived there fourteen years in the so-called Cellia, eating but a pound of bread,[348] and a pint of oil in the space of three months, and he was a man who had been delicately reared in a refined and fastidious manner of life. He composed one hundred prayers, and he wrote during the year only the price of as much as he ate,[349] for he wrote very gracefully the Oxyrhynchus character.[350] Within fifteen years he had so purified his mind that he was deemed worthy of the gift of knowledge and wisdom and the discernment of spirits. Then he drew up three holy books for monks—Controversies[351] they are called—on the arts to be used against demons.

11. The demon of fornication bothered him so oppressively, as he himself told us, that he stood naked throughout the night in a well. It was winter at the time and his flesh froze. And at another time it was the spirit of blasphemy which tormented him. For forty days he never entered a house, as he told us, and his body grew welts in the same way brute animals do. Three demons disguised as

clerics attacked him in broad daylight and they examined him as regards the faith; one said he was an Arian,[352] one an Eunomian,[353] and the third said he was an Apollinarian.[354] He got around them with his knowledge and a few words.

12. Another day when the church key was lost, he made the Sign of the Cross in front of the lock and, giving it a push with his hand, he opened it, calling upon Christ. He was beaten by demons and sorely tempted by them times without number. He told one of his disciples everything that would come to pass after eighteen years, and it came about as he had prophesied.

He said: "I did not touch lettuce or any vegetable greens, or fruit, or grapes, nor did I even take a bath, since the time I came to the desert."

13. Later, in the sixteenth year of living this way without cooked food, his body required food prepared over a fire, because of his weak stomach. He did not take bread, but partook of herbs or barley gruel or porridge for two years. This was his way of life, and he died after having communicated in the church at Epiphany.

Near the time of his death he said: "This is the third year that I am not tormented by carnal desires"—this after a life of such toil and labor and continual prayer! To the one who brought him the news of the death of his father he said: "Stop blaspheming, for my Father is deathless."[355]

39. PIOR

1. Pior[356] was a young Egyptian who bade farewell to his father's house and left. He promised God in an excess of zeal that he would never again see any of his relatives.[357]

After fifty years his sister, grown old by this time, heard that he was still alive; and she was about to break down if she did not see him. Unable herself to go to see him in the Great Desert, she entreated the local bishop to write to the fathers in the desert[358] that they should send him so she might see him. Such force was put upon him that he thought it best to take someone with him and go.

2. At his sister's house it was announced: "Your brother Pior has come." Standing outside he knew from the sound of the door that the old woman had come out for the visit. He closed his eyes and called out to her: "You there! Look here! I am Pior your brother. Here I am. Look at me as long as you like."

She was fully satisfied and she gave praise to God. When she could not persuade him to come into her house, she went back inside. But he prayed at the threshold and went back again to the desert.

3. This marvel is related of him: He dug a well in the place where he lived and found the water most bitter. Yet he lived there until he died, accepting the bitterness of the water so that he might show the power of his endurance. After his death a good many monks strove to rival him by staying in his cell, but they could not finish out a year, for the place is terrible and without one redeeming feature.

4. Moses, the Libyan,[359] was a very gentle and exceedingly lovable man who was accounted worthy of the gift of healing. He told me: "When I was a youth in the monastery we dug a large cistern twenty feet across. Eighty of us had been digging away there for three days and we had gone about a cubit farther than usual. We had expected to find a spring but had not found water. Deeply disappointed, we were considering giving up the task. Pior

happened along then from the Great Desert at the sixth hour, in the heat of the day, and the old man was wearing a cloak. He greeted us and then said: 'Why have you become faint of heart, O ye of little faith?[360] For since yesterday I have seen you losing heart.'

5. "And he went down into the pit of the cistern on a ladder and prayed along with them. He took up the pick-axe and said while striking his third blow: 'O God of the holy Patriarchs,[361] do not bring to naught the labor of your servants, but send them the water they need.' And at once water spouted forth so as to sprinkle them. Then he said another prayer and left. They tried to get him to eat; he did not accede to their wishes, however, but said: 'That for which I was sent is accomplished; I was not sent for this.' "[362]

40. EPHRAEM

1. Surely you have heard about Ephraem,[363] the deacon of the church at Edessa.[364] He happens to be one of those worthy to be commemorated by holy men. He had accomplished the journey of the Spirit in a right and worthy manner, never deviating from the straight path, and he was deemed worthy of the gift of natural knowledge. The knowledge of God succeeded this, and finally blessedness.[365] He always practiced the quiet life and edified those whom he met for many years, but finally he left his cell for the following reason:

2. When a great famine befell the city of Edessa he had compassion for the whole countryside which was being ravaged, and he went to those who were well-to-do and spoke to them: "Why do you not have pity on the people

who are perishing, instead of letting your wealth rot[366] for the condemnation of your own souls?"

They looked about and said: "We have no one whom we should trust to care for those suffering from famine, for all of them make it into a business."

He asked: "How do I seem to you?" For he had a great reputation among them, not for evil, but for good.

3. They said: "We know that you are a man of God."

"Why do you not trust me?" he asked. "Look, I will appoint myself your guestmaster."

And he took money and divided up the porticoes, and he put up about three hundred beds and cared for the famished ones. The dead he buried, and he took care of those who had hope of life, and as a matter of fact he daily provided refreshment and help to all those who came to him each day because of the famine; and this he did with the money allotted to him.

4. When the year was over and prosperity followed and they had all gone back home, he had no more to do. He went back to his cell and died within the month. God had given him this chance for a crown at the very end. He left some writings, too, most of which are worthy of attention.

41. SAINTLY WOMEN[367]

1. I must also commemorate in this book the courageous women[368] to whom God granted struggles equal to those of men, so that no one could plead as an excuse that women are too weak to practice virtue successfully. Now I have seen a good many of them and I have associated with refined women among virgins and widows.

[2. Among these was the Roman matron Paula,[369] who was mother of Toxotius,[370] a woman highly distinguished in the spiritual life. A certain Jerome[371] from Dalmatia stood in her way, for she was well able to surpass everyone else, being a genius of a woman. He thwarted her with his jealousy and prevailed upon her to work to his own end and purpose. She had a daughter, too, who is now an ascetic at Bethlehem. Her name is Eustochium;[372] I never met her myself, but she is said to be very modest and to have a company of fifty virgins.

3. I knew Veneria, too, the wife of Vallovicus[373] the count;[374] she distributed her camel's load[375] very wisely and thus was released from the disappointments which accompany wealth. There was Theodora,[376] too, wife of the tribune, who became so poor that she took alms; she finally died in the monastery of Hesychas[377] by the sea. I knew a woman called Hosia,[378] a most renowned woman in every way, and her sister Adolia,[379] who while not living as worthily as Hosia did, lived at least as worthily as she could by her own means.

4. I knew Basianillia,[380] too, the wife of Candidianus[381] the general; she practiced virtue zealously and carefully and still is vigorously fighting the good fight. And I knew Photeina,[382] too, a maiden of the highest renown, a daughter of Theoctistus,[383] the priest of Laodicea. And in Antioch I came across a woman also of great renown who held converse intimately with God, the deaconess Sabiniana,[384] aunt of John, bishop of Constantinople. And in Rome I also saw the fair Asella,[385] a virgin grown old in the monastery, an exceedingly meek woman and one who was a help to the convent.

5. Among them I saw both men and women newly

instructed. I saw Abita,[386] too, the saint of God, who with her husband Apronianus[387] and their daughter Eunomia,[388] desirous to please God, was converted openly to a virtuous and temperate way of life. For this they were deemed worthy to sleep in Christ, free of every sin and full of knowledge, leaving their lives in good remembrance.]

42. JULIAN

I heard of one Julian[389] in the vicinity of Edessa, a man most ascetic, who mortified his flesh excessively and was reduced to skin and bones. At the close of his life he was deemed worthy of the honor of the gift of healing.

43. ADOLIUS

1. I also knew Adolius[390] at Jerusalem. He was a Tarsian by birth who had come to Jerusalem by an altogether different way, not at all by the way we traveled, but cut out for himself a strange way of life. For his ascetic practice was beyond man to such a degree that the very demons trembled at his strictness of life and no one dared to rival him. Because of his excessive self-control and all-night vigils he was actually suspected of being a monster.

2. For in Lent he would eat only every five days, although at other times he ate every other day. But the big thing he did was this: From the time of evening until the brotherhood gathered again in its house of prayer, he would stand on the Mount of Olives, on the Hill of Ascension, the place where Jesus was taken up. There he would stand, singing psalms and praying, and even if it

snowed or rained, or there was a frost, he would remain there unshaken.

3. After he had completed his usual time he would knock at the cells of all with the clapper he used in waking them. He would bring them together in houses for prayer and at each oratory join them in singing one or two psalms antiphonally.[391] After he had prayed with them he would go off to his cell before it was day. As a matter of fact the brethren often undressed him, wrung out his clothes as though they were just from the laundry, and put others on him. So then he would rest until the hour of psalmody, and he would keep busy until evening. This, then, was the virtue of Adolius the Tarsian who attained perfection in Jerusalem and there went to sleep.

44. INNOCENT

1. You have heard from many all about the blessed Innocent,[392] the priest of the Mount of Olives; nevertheless you will also hear from us, who lived with him for three years. He was simple beyond measure. He had been one of the palace dignitaries in the early days of Emperor Constantius. He left the world, leaving his marriage by which he had a son, Paul, one of the royal bodyguard.

2. When his son had wronged the daughter of a priest, Innocent cursed him and called upon God, saying: "O Lord, give this man a spirit that he may no longer find a chance for sinning against the flesh."[393] He thought it was better that his son fight with a demon than against impurity. This indeed happened, and the son is still in irons on the Mount of Olives being punished by the spirit.

3. This Innocent was so kindhearted that I shall seem silly when I tell the truth. Often he himself stole from the brethren and gave to those in need. He was extremely guileless and simple and was deemed worthy of the gift of power against demons. Once we ourselves saw brought to him a young man who was paralyzed and possessed. I reprimanded the young man's mother for bringing him, as I doubted that he could be cured.

4. Meanwhile the old man chanced to come up and see her standing there weeping and bewailing the unspeakable misfortune of her son. Then the venerable old man wept; deeply moved, he took the young man into the shrine which he himself had erected and in which were kept the relics of Saint John the Baptist. And he prayed over him from the third to the ninth hour and then returned him healed to his mother the same day, as he had driven out both the paralysis and the demon. The paralysis had been of such a form that when the young man spat, he spat upon his own back, so turned about he was.

5. A certain old lady missed her sheep and came to him weeping. He followed her and said: "Show me where you lost your sheep." She led him near the place of Lazarus.[394] He stood there and prayed. Now the young men who were guilty had killed the sheep when they anticipated capture. He prayed, but no one confessed. The meat was hidden in the vineyard. A crow coming from some place alighted, took a piece, and was off again. The blessed one observed this and found the slaughtered victim. Then the young men fell down and confessed to having killed it, and they paid the just price for it.

45. PHILOROMUS

1. In Galatia we met with the priest Philoromus,[395] a most ascetic and patient man. He was born of a mother who was a household slave and a father who was a free-man, but he showed such nobility in his Christian life that even those of irreproachable stock honored him for his life and virtue.

He left the world in the days of Julian, that hateful emperor,[396] and he used to speak up to him boldly. Julian ordered him to be shaved and cuffed about by mere boys; this he endured as nothing unusual and he even thanked Julian for it, as he himself related.

2. In his early days he underwent the battle of impurity and gluttony, which he drove out by confining himself in irons and by abstaining from wheaten bread and anything that had been cooked on a fire. He endured all these things for eighteen years and then sang the triumphal ode of Christ. He was warred against by spirits of evil for forty years in one monastery. He used to tell us that "for thirty-two years I partook of no fruit." Once when cowardice plagued him, he confined himself to a tomb for six years.

3. Finally Saint Basil the Bishop[397] looked after him, pleased at his austerity and perseverance. He had not yet stopped writing although he was eighty years old. He said that "from the time I was first initiated and born again on up to the present time, I have never eaten from another's hand without charge but have eaten only that which I got by my own labor."[398] As though before God Himself he convinced us that he had given two hundred and fifty

coins to cripples out of his own hand and that he had never wronged anyone.

4. He journeyed on foot even to Rome itself with the intention of praying at the shrine of Saint Peter. He went to Alexandria to pray at the shrine of Mark.[399] On a second trip he went to Jerusalem on foot, paying his own expenses. He used to say: "Never do I remember being absent from God in thought."

46. MELANIA THE ELDER

1. Melania[400] the thrice blessed was Spanish by birth and later a Roman. She was the daughter[401] of Marcellinus, one of the consuls,[402] and wife of some man of high rank, I forget which. She was widowed at twenty-two and was counted worthy of divine love, and she told no one, for she would have been stopped at that time, when Valens[403] held rule. She had a trustee named for her son, and taking every movable piece of her property she put it on board ship and set off for Alexandria at full speed with illustrious women and children.[404]

2. And there she sold her possessions and changed her holdings into gold. She went to Mount Nitria and met Pambo,[405] Arsisius,[406] Sarapion[407] the Great, Paphnutius of Scete,[408] Isidore the Confessor,[409] and Dioscorus,[410] bishop of Hermopolis. And she spent up to half a year with them, making the rounds of the desert and seeking out all the holy men.

3. Subsequently the Augustial prefect[411] banished Isidore, Pisimius, Adelphius,[412] Paphnutius, and Pambo, as well as Ammonius Parotes[413] along with them, and twelve bishops and priests, to Palestine near Diocaesarea. She fol-

lowed them and served them from her own private treasury. Now they said they were not allowed servants[414] (I happened to meet the holy Pisimius and Isidore and Paphnutius and Ammonius), so she wore a slave's hood[415] and used to bring them what they needed at evening. Now the consul of Palestine knew of this, and desiring to fill his pocket he decided to blackmail her.

4. He seized her and cast her into prison, not knowing that she was a freewoman.

But she made it clear to him: "I am So-and-so's daughter and So-and-so's wife. I am Christ's slave. Pray do not look down upon my shabby clothes, for I could make more of myself if I would. I have made this clear to you so that you may not fall under legal charges without knowing the reason"—for one must use the sagacity of a hawk where insensate people are concerned![416]

The judge then realized the situation; he apologized to her and paid her respect, and he ordered that she could associate with the holy men without hindrance.

5. After they were recalled from exile, she built a monastery in Jerusalem and lived there twenty-seven years heading a company of fifty virgins. Close by dwelt also the very noble Rufinus[417] from the Italian city of Aquileia; his way of life was like hers, and he was a most staunch man, later deemed worthy of the priesthood—a more learned and reasonable man was never found.[418]

6. So for twenty-seven years they both entertained with their own private funds the bishops, solitaries, and virgins who visited them, coming to Jerusalem to fulfil a vow. They edified all their visitors and united the four hundred monks of the Pauline schism by persuading every heretic who denied the Holy Spirit[419] and so brought them

back to the Church. They bestowed gifts and food on the local clergy, and so finished their days without offending anyone.

47. CHRONIUS AND PAPHNUTIUS

1. One by the name of Chronius[420] from the village called Phoinice[421] measured off 15,000 steps[422] from his own village, which was close to the desert, and there he prayed and dug a well. He found fresh water six fathoms[423] down. He built himself a small hut there. After he had established himself there, he prayed God that he would never again return to an inhabited place.

2. When a few years had gone by and there had gathered around him a brotherhood of some two hundred men, he was deemed worthy of the priesthood. This virtue of his asceticism is related, namely, that, having served the altar for sixty years in his priestly function, he did not leave the desert nor did he eat any bread that was not the product of his own labor. Together with him lived a certain James, one of the neighbors surnamed the Halt,[424] learned in a high degree. Both of them were acquainted with the blessed Antony.

3. One day Paphnutius,[425] who was also called Kephalas, joined them. He had the gift of divine knowledge of Sacred Scripture, both the Old and the New Testament, explaining them without ever having read the writings,[426] but he was so meek that his prophetic gift was hidden. Of him it is reported that in eighty years he never wore two tunics at once. When the blessed Evagrius[427] and Albanius[428] and I met such men as these, we sought to learn

why brethren should go astray, or leave, or be frustrated in the proper life.

4. For it happened in those days that Chaeremon[429] the ascetic had died sitting up and was found dead in his chair holding his work in his hands. And again another brother was covered up while digging a well. Still another who was coming down from Scete died from lack of water. Then, too, we have Stephen,[430] who fell into shameful libertinism, and also the story of Eucarpius[431] and of Heron[432] of Alexandria, as well as Valens[433] of Palestine and Ptolemy the Egyptian[434] in Scete.

5. Then together we asked why it was that men living in the desert sometimes are deceived in their minds or are wrecked by lust.

Paphnutius, the most learned man, then answered us as follows:[435] "Everything that comes about is one of two things, that which God approves or that which He permits. Everything that happens which is in accordance with virtue and the glory of God happens by His will. Now, on the other hand, things harmful and dangerous, accidents and falls, these occur with God's consent.

6. "Now His consent comes about reasonably; for it is impossible that one who thinks and acts rightly could fall into disgrace or into the trap of demons. Then those who seem to practice virtue but have a debased purpose, or have the fault of acting to please their fellow men or the vice of a willful imagination, these also fall into errors, as God abandons them for their own good, so that through the symptoms they may perceive the change and so correct themselves in both intention and act.

7. "For at times people sin in the will, acting with evil

intent, but at other times they sin in conduct also, when they act through corruption or in evil fashion. Now it often happens that an evil man with a bad intention gives alms to young women for an evil end. On the other hand, it is a quite praiseworthy thing to give succor to an orphan, to a solitary, or to one who practices the ascetic life. It is also possible for one to give alms with a right intention to the sick or the aged, or to those who have lost money, but to do it sparingly and with grumbling; the intention is right, but the act is not worthy of the intention, for the merciful man ought to give alms *with cheerfulness*[436] and with generosity."

8. They also said this: "There are superior abilities in many souls. Some have a natural ability for meditation; others have a readiness for ascetic practices. But whenever an action or some naturally good act is not done for the sake of the good end itself, or when those who have superior abilities attribute them not to God, the dispenser of all good things, but to their own will and goodness and self-sufficiency, these persons are abandoned completely and given over either to shameless conduct or to shameful experiences. Because of the resultant humiliation and shame they slowly rid themselves of the pride they have in their pretended virtue.

9. "For when a person is swollen with pride and magnifies the charm of his own speeches, and attributes his charm or the abundance of his knowledge not to God but to his own ascetic practices or his own knowledge, then God removes the Angel of Providence from him. When the angel is removed, then he is distressed by the Adversary and brags of his own natural ability, and thus falls into impurity through his overweening pride. So, the

witness of his own prudence is taken away, and what is spoken by him[437] is not worthy of credence—in fact pious men flee the teaching coming from the mouth of such a one as though it were a spring with leeches. So the Holy Scriptures are fulfilled: *But to the sinner God hath said: Why dost thou declare my justices, and take my covenant in thy mouth?*[438]

10. "For, to be sure, the souls of the sinful resemble different fountains. The gluttons and lovers of wine resemble springs that have been fouled; the greedy and fraudulent are like fountains with frogs; the envious and arrogant who yet have some habits of knowledge are similar to springs inhabited by serpents in which reason stagnates, for no one willingly draws benefit out of them because of the bitterness of their character. Hence David asked for three things when praying: *goodness and discipline and knowledge,*[439] for knowledge without goodness is not good.

11. "But should such a man correct himself, and put away the cause of his dereliction, namely his pride, and should he regain humility and realize his proper worth, and stop putting himself above his neighbor, and be thankful to God, then knowledge with its own proofs comes back again. For spiritual words not shared with one who lives a holy and prudent life are as corn blasted by the wind; they have the appearance, but their nutriment is stolen away.[440]

12. "Then every fall, whether in tongue, in feeling, in deed, or in the entire body, leads to abandonment, and this is greater as the pride is greater; but God has consideration for the ones who are abandoned. For should the Lord give testimony to their natural talent by eloquent speech, their

pride would make them into demons swollen in their impurity."

13. And these same men told us this also: "When you see a man of vulgar life who is nevertheless a persuasive speaker, think of the demon who while conversing with Christ quoted Holy Scripture, and of the witness which says: *Now the serpent was more subtle than any of the beasts of the earth.*[441] Now the subtlety of the serpent could lead only to harm, since it had no other good feature but this. For the faithful and good man must think the thoughts sent by God; he must speak what he thinks and act according to what he says.

14. "For if the way a person lives is not in accord with the truth of his words, then such a person is like bread without salt, as Job says, which either is not eaten at all or, if eaten, will lead to bodily illness. *For,* he says, *is bread eaten without salt?*[442] And is there taste in empty words, which are not fulfilled by testimony of the deed? Now this is why these people are abandoned; so that the virtue which was hidden might be made known, as was Job's virtue when God answered him, saying:

" '*Wilt thou make void my judgment? And condemn me, that thou mayest be justified?*[443]

15. " 'For you were known to Me, who see the hidden things, but you were not known to men, who suspected that you served Me for riches. I brought on the crisis, I cut off the riches in order that I might show them that your philosophy is pleasing to Me.'

"It is to overthrow pride, as in the case of Paul; for he was abandoned, tossed about in misfortunes and buffetings, and in various tribulations, and he said: *There was given me a sting to my flesh, an angel of Satan to buffet me, lest I be exalted.*[444]

16. "That is to say, so that the repose and prosperity and honor which were heaped upon him because of these miracles might not drive him to conceit like the devil's and puff him up with pride. Through his own fault the paralytic was abandoned, since Jesus said: *Behold, thou art made whole, sin no more.*[445] Judas, too, was abandoned, because he preferred money to the Word—that is why he hanged. And Esau was abandoned and fell into evil because he preferred the filth of intestines to his father's blessing.[446]

17. "Thus all these things are taken into account when Paul speaks of some: *And as they liked not to have God in their knowledge, God delivered them up to a reprobate sense, to do those things which are not convenient;*[447] and to certain others who appear to have knowledge of God with a debased mind: *Because that, when they know God, they have not glorified Him as God or given thanks.*[448] *For this cause God delivered them up to shameful afflictions.*[449]

"From this, then, we may know that it is impossible for anyone to fall into sin unless he has been abandoned by God's providence."

48. ELPIDIUS

1. There lived a certain Elpidius[450] in the caves near Jericho which the Amorites had hewed out of rock when they fled Josue, son of Nun,[451] when he plundered the foreign tribes on the mountain of Ducas.[452] He was a Cappadocian, and he was some time later deemed worthy of

the priesthood and became chorbishop of the monastery of Timotheus[453] the Cappadocian, himself a very able man. When he came there he dwelt in one of the caves. He displayed such self-control in his ascetic practices that he overshadowed all the rest.

2. He lived there twenty-five years, eating only on Sundays and Saturdays, and he stood up all night singing psalms. He was like a king of the bees[454] in the midst of the brotherhood dwelling there, and I lived there, too. He transformed the mountain into a city and one could see various types of living there. One night a scorpion bit this Elpidius as he was chanting psalms. We were singing along with him. He stamped his foot on it and never even shifted his stance, having no regard for the scorpion's bite.

3. One day a brother was holding a piece of vine-cutting and he took it, sitting where he was on the slope of the mountain, and heaped dirt up over it as though planting it. Although it was not the right season, the cutting grew into a vine so large it covered the church. Along with him Aenesius,[455] a praiseworthy man, attained perfection, as did his brother Eustathius.[456] He reached such a high degree of mortification and so wasted away his body that the sun shone through his bones.

4. This story is told by his earnest disciples: He never looked westward because the mountain at the door of his cave blocked the view. Nor could he see the sun after the sixth hour because of the height of the mountain on the west side, nor did he see the stars which appear on the western horizon—not for twenty-five years! Once he entered his cave he never came down the mountain until he was buried.

49. SISINNIUS

1. Sisinnius[457] was a disciple of this Elpidius. He was a slave by birth, but free by faith, a Cappadocian by race; for one should mention these things for the glory of Christ who uplifts us and leads us to true nobility. He spent six or seven years with Elpidius and afterwards confined himself to a tomb. He spent three years in prayer in the tomb, sitting down neither at night nor in the day; nor did he lie down or go outside. He was deemed worthy of the gift against demons.

2. Now he went back to his country and was deemed worthy of the priesthood, and he gathered together a brotherhood of men and women. By his revered way of life he drove out his own masculine desires, and by his mastery he bridled the feminine traits of the women, so that the Scriptures are fulfilled: *In Christ Jesus there is neither male nor female.*[458] He is hospitable to strangers even though he has no property, a reproach to the rich who do not share their wealth.[459]

50. GADDANES

I knew an old Palestinian, Gaddanes[460] by name, who lived his life with no roof over his head in the vicinity of the Jordan. Once some Jews around the Dead Sea set upon him in their zeal and approached him baring their swords. And the following incident occurred: As one raised his sword and was on the point of turning it against Gaddanes, his hand was withered up and the sword fell from him.

51. ELIAS

1. There was Elias,[461] too, who lived as a solitary in a cave in this vicinity. He led a most holy life of self-control. One day a good many brethren visited him, for the place was along the road, and he ran out of bread. And he assured us: "At my wit's end I entered the cell and found three loaves. There were twenty of them. When they had eaten enough, one loaf remained. This furnished me food for twenty-five days."

52. SABAS

There was one named Sabas,[462] a secular,[463] a married man of Jericho, who became such a friend of the monks that he made the rounds of the cells and the desert by night and left at each cell a peck[464] of dates and a supply of vegetables, for the ascetics along the Jordan do not eat bread. One day he was met by a lion. It caught up with him after a way, gave him a shove and threw him over, and then made off with his mule.

53. ABRAMIUS

A certain Abramius,[465] of Egyptian descent, lived a most harsh and rough life in the desert. He was smitten in his mind with troublesome self-conceit; he went to church and argued with the priests, and he said: "I was ordained priest just this past night by Christ; now allow me to perform the functions of a priest."

The fathers took him away from the desert and brought him to a less ascetic and less exacting way of life, and they cured this man of his arrogance by bringing him, who had been the sport of demons, to a knowledge of his own weakness.

54. MORE ABOUT MELANIA THE ELDER

1. I have told above in an offhand way of the wondrous and holy Melania.[466] Nevertheless I shall weave into this account some remaining features. So much wealth did she spend in holy zeal, consumed in a fire as it were, that not I but those rather who inhabit Persia should give the account.[467] No one failed to benefit by her good works, neither in the east nor in the west, neither in the north nor in the south.[468]

2. For thirty-seven years she practiced hospitality; from her own treasury she made donations to churches, monasteries, guests, and prisons. Her own family and son[469] and stewards provided the funds for this. She persisted in her hospitality to such an extent that she had not even a span[470] of earth for herself, nor did she permit yearning for her son to separate her from love toward Christ,[471] although she had but one son.

3. But because of her prayers the young man attained a high degree of education and character, made a good marriage, and became great by worldly standards. He even had two children. A long time afterwards she heard how her granddaughter was doing—how she had married and then elected to leave the world. She feared that they might be utterly destroyed by bad teaching or heresy or bad living; although she was already an old woman of sixty, she boarded a boat at Caesarea and sailed for twenty days to Rome.[472]

4. And there she met with a most holy and remarkable man, a Greek named Apronianus,[473] whom she instructed and made a Christian. She even prevailed upon him to exert self-control concerning his own wife Abita, who was her cousin. She lent moral support to her own granddaughter Melania and to the latter's husband Pinianus[474] as well, and she even taught her son's wife Albina.[475] She induced them to sell their goods, and she led them away from Rome and brought them to the haven of a holy and calm life.

5. When she did this she was actually fighting beasts[476] —I mean the members of the Senate and their wives, who would have stood in the way of their renunciation. But she said: "*Little children*, it was written over four hundred years ago, *it is the last hour*.[477] Why are you fond of the vain things of life? Beware lest the days of the Antichrist overtake you and you not enjoy your wealth and your ancestral property."

6. Now she freed all these and led them to the solitary life. She taught the younger son of Publicola[478] and led him to Sicily. She sold everything which remained, and with the money she received she went to Jerusalem. Then she distributed her wealth within forty days and fell asleep in fine old age, in the deepest meekness. She left a monastery at Jerusalem, too, and funds for it.

7. When they had all left Rome, a barbarian deluge,[479] mentioned long before in prophecy,[480] fell upon Rome. Even the bronze statues in the Forum did not escape, for everything was plundered and destroyed with barbarian fury. Thus Rome, beautifully adorned for twelve hundred years, became a ruin. Then those who had been Melania's pupils, as well as those who had been opposed to

the instruction, gave praise to God, who had convinced the unbelievers by a turn of events; when all the others were taken prisoner, those alone were saved who had become holocaust for the Lord through Melania's zealousness.[481]

55. SILVANIA[482]

1. It happened that we made a journey from Aelia[483] to Egypt, sending off the blessed Silvania,[484] the maiden sister-in-law of Rufinus the ex-prefect. Jovinus[485] also was with us; he was a deacon at the time but is now bishop of the Church at Ascalon,[486] a pious and well-learned man. The weather was terribly hot for us, and when we arrived at Pelusium,[487] Jovinus took a basin and gave his hands and feet a thorough washing in very cold water.[488] Afterwards he lay down to rest on a leather cushion thrown on the ground.

2. Melania[489] approached him like a wise mother approaching her own son, and she scoffed at his weakness, saying: "How can a warm-blooded young man like you dare to pamper your flesh that way? Do you not know that this is the source of much harm? Look, I am sixty years old and neither my feet nor my face, nor any of my members, except for the tips of my fingers, has touched water, although I am afflicted with many ailments and my doctors urge me. I have not yet made concessions to my bodily desires, nor have I used a couch for resting, nor have I ever made a journey on a litter."

3. She was most erudite and fond of literature,[490] and she turned night into day going through every writing of the ancient commentators—three million lines of Origen and two and a half million lines of Gregory, Stephen,

Pierius,[491] Basil, and other worthy men. And she did not
read them once only and in an offhand way, but she worked
on them, dredging through each work seven or eight times.
Thus it was possible for her to be liberated from *knowledge falsely so called*[492] and to mount on wings, thanks to
those books—by good hopes she transformed herself into a
spiritual bird and so made the journey to Christ.

56. OLYMPIAS

1. The most revered and emulous Olympias[493] followed her commands both in her memory and in her very
footsteps. She was the daughter of Seleucus,[494] one of the
ex-counts,[495] and granddaughter of Ablavius[496] the ex-prefect, and for a few days a bride of Nebridius,[497] one of the
ex-prefects of the city, but she was no man's wife. They
say that she died a virgin, wife only of the Word of
Truth.

2. She disposed of all her goods, giving them to the
needy.[498] She took part in no small contests on the behalf
of truth, instructed many women, addressed priests with
reverence, paid honor to bishops, and was deemed worthy
to be a confessor on behalf of truth. Those who live at
Constantinople number her among the confessors. She
died and traveled on to the Lord in her struggles for God.

57. CANDIDA AND GELASIA

1. The blessed Candida,[499] daughter of the general Trajan,[500] followed in her footsteps, as though mirroring her.
She lived worthily and attained the highest degree of
sanctity, holding in honor both the churches and bish-

ops.[501] She gave instruction to her own daughter for the vocation of chastity, giving her to Christ as the gift of her own womb, afterwards following her in moderation and in the distribution of her wealth.

2. I knew her to spend the whole night at the mill toiling with her hands to bring her body into subjection. She would say: "Fasting is not sufficient. I supply an ally, namely toilsome wakefulness, so that I may destroy the arrogance of Esau."[502] She abstained completely from anything warm-blooded or animate, but she partook of fish and vegetables with oil on feast days, and otherwise satisfied herself with a little sour wine and dry bread.

3. Following in her example in pious fashion went the most renowned Gelasia,[503] daughter of a tribune who had put on the yoke of virginity. Her virtue was said to be such that the sun never set on her anger,[504] not even at manservant or handmaid.

58. THE MONKS OF ANTINOE

1. I spent four years in Antinoë[505] in the Thebaid and in that time I gained a knowledge of the monasteries there. About twelve hundred men dwell around the city living by the toil of their hands and practicing asceticism to a high degree. Among them there are also anchorites who have confined themselves in rocky caves.

Solomon[506] was one of these, a most mild man, sensible, and one who had the gift of endurance. He said that he was fifty years in the cave. He kept himself supplied by the work of his own hands and he had learned all the Holy Scriptures by heart.

2. Dorotheus,[507] a priest, lived in another cave, perfect in a high degree, and he led a completely blameless life. He was deemed worthy of the priesthood and performed the priestly functions for the brethren in the caves. Once Melania, the granddaughter of the great Melania, of whom I shall speak below,[508] sent him five hundred coins, begging him to officiate for the brethren there. He took but three of the coins and sent the rest to Diocles[509] the anchorite, a most learned man, saying: "Brother Diocles is wiser than I and can minister to them without harm, for he knows their needs better; I am quite satisfied with these."

3. This Diocles began with grammar at first, then gave himself over to philosophy. All this time grace was attracting him, and at twenty-eight he left the study of the liberal arts[510] and joined himself to Christ. He had spent thirty-five years in the caves. He addressed us as follows: "Mind divorced from the thought of God becomes either a demon or a brute."

Then since we inquired to know what he had said, he told us: "Mind divorced from the thought of God necessarily falls into desire or anger." He explained that desire was beastlike, but anger was demonlike.

4. When I raised an objection, asking how a man's mind could always be with God, he answered: "Whenever the soul is concerned with a thought or deed that is pious or godlike, then it is with God."

Near him dwelt Capiton,[511] a former robber.[512] He lived fifty years in the caves about four miles from the deme of Antinoë and he did not descend from his cave or approach the Nile River. He said that he could not yet associate with crowds as the Enemy would still oppose him.

5. We also saw another anchorite among them living like him in a cave. He was deluded in dreams by the madness of vainglory; then he mocked those who were themselves deceived, *feeding the winds*.[513] Yet he held his body in check, both because of his age and the season, perhaps also because of his vainglory.[514] However, his thinking powers were utterly deranged by the great evil of vainglory.

59. AMMA TALIS AND TAOR

1. In the town of Antinoë are twelve monasteries of women. Here I met Amma Talis,[515] a woman eighty years old in the ascetic life, as her neighbors affirmed. Sixty young women lived with her. They loved her so much that no lock was placed in the hall of the monastery, as in others, but they were held in check by their love for her. The old woman had such a high degree of self-control that when I had entered and taken a seat, she came and sat with me and placed her hands on my shoulders in a burst of frankness.

2. In this monastery was a maiden, a disciple of hers named Taor,[516] who had spent thirty years there. She was never willing to take a new garment, hood, or shoes, but said: "I have no need for them unless I must go out." The others all go out every Sunday to church for Communion,[517] but she stays behind in her cell dressed in rags, ever sitting at her work. She is so graceful in appearance that even a well-controlled person might be led astray by her beauty were not chastity her defense and did not her decorum turn sinful eyes to fear and shame.

60. THE VIRGIN AND COLLUTHUS THE MARTYR

1. There was another neighbor of mine whose face I never beheld, for she never went out, so they say, from the time when she left the world. She had completed sixty years in ascetic practices along with her mother and at last she was on the point of passing to the next world. And the martyr of that place, Colluthus by name,[518] stood over her and said: "This day you will make the journey to the Master and see all the saints. Come, then, and eat with us in the chapel."[519]

She arose then at dawn, dressed, and took in her basket bread, olives, and chopped vegetables. After all these years she went out and she entered the chapel and prayed.

2. Then she watched the whole day for an opportunity when no one was within, and taking her seat, she addressed the martyr: "Bless my food, O holy Colluthus, and help me on my journey with your prayers."

She ate and prayed again, and she went back home about sunset. She gave her mother a composition of Clement the Stromatist[520] on the prophet Amos[521] and said: "Give it to the banished bishop[522] and tell him to pray for me, for I am on my journey."

And she died that night, without fever or delirium, but laid out for burial.[523]

61. MELANIA THE YOUNGER

1. Since I promised above[524] to tell you about the daughter of Melania,[525] I must fulfill my promise, for it is

not right that we overlook her tender age and disregard such virtue, which is commemorated without a memorial and which as a matter of fact excelled that of even elderly women far advanced in holiness. Her parents forced her into an early marriage with a man of one of the first families in Rome. She was continually stung by the stories about her grandmother and she was so chagrined that she could not cooperate with him in marriage.

2. Two sons were born, but they both died. She came to find marriage so hateful that she said to her husband Pinianus,[526] the son of Severus the ex-prefect:[527] "If you prefer to practice asceticism in company with me by an agreement to chastity, then I will recognize you as master and as lord of my life. If this seems too hard to you, for you are a young man, take what is mine, but set my body free so that I may fulfill my will to God and enter into my inheritance of the zeal of my grandmother whose name I bear.

3. "For had God willed us to have children, He would not have taken away my children so soon."

For a time then they fought against the yoke, but finally God took mercy on the young man and implanted in him a desire to leave the world. Thus so far as they were concerned were the Scriptures fulfilled: *For how knowest thou, O wife, whether thou shalt save thy husband?*[528]

Now she had been married at thirteen and lived with her husband for seven years, and at twenty she left the world. And first of all she gave away her silken garments to the sanctuary;[529] the holy Olympias had done likewise.

4. She divided up the rest of her silks and made various church decorations. Her silver and gold she entrusted to Paul, a certain priest, a Dalmatian monk.[530] She sent

across the sea to the East ten thousand pieces of money to Egypt and the Thebaid, ten thousand to Antioch and the vicinity thereof, fifteen thousand to Palestine, ten thousand to the churches in the Islands and beyond; she likewise made donations to the churches in the West.

5. All this and four times as much in addition did she rescue *from the mouth of the lion*[531]—I mean Alaric,[532] if God will forgive the expression. Her own faith led her to set free eight thousand slaves who desired freedom. The rest of the slaves did not want this, however, choosing rather to serve her brother, to whom she sold them for three pieces of money. She sold off everything she had in Spain, Aquitania, Taraconia, and Gaul, keeping for endowment of the monasteries only her holdings in Sicily, Campania, and Africa.

6. That was her wisdom in regard to the burden of riches. This was her asceticism: She ate every other day, but in the beginning of her ascetical life at intervals of more than five days, and she arranged to do herself some of the daily work of her slave women, whom she made her associates in her ascetic practices. She had with her also her mother Albina,[533] who lived a life as ascetic as her own and who had made a private distribution of her own wealth. They are now dwelling in the country, sometimes in Sicily, again in Campania, with fifteen eunuchs[534] and sixty maidens, both freewomen and slaves.

7. In a like manner her husband Pinianus lives with thirty monks reading and engaged in gardening and solemn conferences.[535] They honored us not a little when quite a few of us were on the way to Rome[536] because of Saint John the Bishop.[537] They entertained us with hospitality and abundant provisions for the journey, gaining for them-

selves with great joy the fruit of eternal life by their God-
given works of the best way of life.

62. PAMMACHIUS

Their relative Pammachius[538] likewise bade farewell to
the world and lived the best life and distributed some of
his wealth while still alive, leaving the rest at his death
to the poor. So, too, there was a certain Macarius,[539] an
ex-vicar,[540] as well as Constantius,[541] a colleague who became one of the prefects in Italy. Both of these were also
notable and learned men who progressed to the highest
love of God. I think that they are still alive practicing the
perfect life.

63. ATHANASIUS AND THE YOUNG MAIDEN

1. In Alexandria I knew a virgin whom I met when she
was about seventy years old. All the clergy confirmed
that when she was a young maiden of about twenty she
was exceedingly pretty and really to be avoided because of
her beauty, lest one be suspected of having been with her.
Now it happened that the Arians were in conspiracy
against Saint Athanasius, the Bishop of Alexandria, working through Eusebius while Constantius was Emperor.[542]
They were bringing false charges and accusing Athanasius
of unlawful deeds, and he fled to avoid the risk of being
judged by a corrupt court. He trusted his person to no
one, not to relative, friend, cleric, or anyone else.

2. But when the prefects came suddenly into the bishop's palace looking for him, he fled in the middle of the

night, taking only his tunic and cloak, and went to the maiden. She was astonished and frightened by this.

He told her: "Since the Arians are searching for me and have informed on me unjustly, I made up my mind to flee so that I might not get a bad reputation and be the cause of a crime by those who want to punish me.

3. "Just this night now God made it clear to me that I will be saved by no one but you."

With great joy then she cast all doubts to the wind and became an instrument of the Lord. She hid the most holy man for six years, until the death of Constantius.[543] She washed his feet and cared for all his bodily needs and his personal affairs, obtaining the loan of books for his use. During these six years no one in Alexandria knew where Saint Athanasius was spending his time.

4. When news of the death of Constantius reached him, he got dressed and appeared in the church at night.[544] All were amazed and looked on him as one risen from the dead. Then he explained all to his dear friends: "I did not flee to you, in order that you might be able to swear that you did not know of my whereabouts. It was the same in regard to the search for me. Now I took flight to one who would be the last to be suspected, she being so pretty and young. I paid court[545] to her on two counts, really: her salvation—for it did help her—as well as my own good name."

64. JULIANA

1. Then there was a maiden, Juliana,[546] in Caesarea of Cappadocia, said to be a most learned and trustworthy woman. She took in Origen the writer when he fled from

the insurrection of the pagans,[547] and she kept him at her own expense for two years and looked after him.

This is what I found written in a very old book of verses, and it was written there in Origen's own hand:

2. "I found this book among the things of Juliana the virgin in Caesarea when I was hidden by her. She used to say that she had it from Symmachus[548] himself, the translator of the Jews."[549]

In passing I have put in the virtues of these women so that we may learn that we can gain in many ways if we would.

65. HIPPOLYTUS

1. In another book written long ago and bearing the name of Hippolytus, a man who knew the apostles,[550] I found this tale:[551]

There lived in Corinth a most nobly born and most attractive maiden who was vowed to virginity. One time during the persecutions they handed her over to the pagan[552] judge as one who cursed the times and those in civil authority and even the idols themselves. But those who handle such matters kept talking about her beauty.

2. The judge was libidinous and, like a horse with his ears pricked up, he willingly listened to the informers. He tried with every trick to seduce her. Finally angered, however, he did not sentence her to punishment or death, but rather placed her in a brothel and ordered the one in charge of those there: "Take this woman and pay me three coins a day to hire her out."

But he, wishing to earn this amount, turned her over to any who were willing to use her.[553] Now the lecherous sort of woman-hunters who frequent that kind of place were there and, after paying the fee, spoke to her about what they had in mind.

3. But she entreated them and appealed to them, saying: "I have an ulcer in a hidden place which emits an unpleasant odor and I fear that you will hate me. Give me a few days' grace and it is possible that you can have me for nothing."[554]

Then during those next days she begged God in her prayers. God perceived her virtue and inspired a young man who worked for the master of offices to die the martyr's death. The young man feigned lust, went late at night to the jail-keeper, and, having paid him five coins, said: "Let me stay with her all night."

4. Entering the private room he told her: "Get up and save yourself." He undressed her, had her change into his own clothes, his shirt and tunic, and all his male clothing, and he told her: "Cover yourself completely[555] with the end of the tunic and get out of here." Sealing herself with the Sign of the Cross,[556] she went out in this way, undefiled and with her chastity intact.

The next day the whole business was known. The young man was apprehended and cast to the beasts.[557] Thus the demon was put to shame, for the young man was a martyr on two counts, both for himself and for her.

66. VERUS THE EX-COUNT

1. In the town of Ancyra[558] in Galatia I met with one Verus,[559] a most distinguished man, and I got to know him —an ex-count[560]—and his wife Bosporia[561] quite well.

They came to practice charity to such an extent that

they even cheated their own children, if we look at the future with worldly eyes. For they spent the income from their properties on the needy. Even though they have two daughters and four sons, they gave nothing to them, except for the married daughters, saying: "After we are gone everything of ours will be yours." They received the fruits of their possessions and distributed them to the churches of the cities and towns.

2. This will show their high degree of virtue: When a famine raged they fought against natural affections and helped to bring heretics back to orthodoxy. In many places they made their stores of grain available to the poor. As for all other matters, they lead a very severe and austere life; they wear cheap clothing and live simply, practicing moderation for God's sake, being associated with country life rather than the crowded cities so that they might not fall in the enticing snares of city ways and fall short of their purpose.

67. MAGNA

1. In this same town of Ancyra lived many other virgins, probably two thousand or more. They practiced chastity and were remarkable women indeed. One of them, Magna,[562] was a most revered woman and takes an eminent place among them. I do not know what to call her, whether virgin or widow, for she was forcibly married to a man by her mother, but she deceived him and kept putting him off, as many say, so that she remained intact.

2. When he died not long afterward, she gave herself over completely to God, paying the strictest attention to

her own houses, and she lived a most ascetic and chaste life, keeping her conversation such that even bishops honored her for her excellent piety. She gave money for hospitals, for the poor, and for bishops on pilgrimages, never ceasing from work. She did this in secret through her most trusted servants, and at night she never left the church.

68. THE COMPASSIONATE MONK

1. Also in this very same city we found a monk who preferred not to be ordained to the priesthood. He had spent some time in the army and had now spent twenty years as an ascetic. He lived with the bishop of the town. So great was his mercy and so kind was he that he went about at night and had mercy on the needy.

2. He neglected neither the prison nor the hospital, neither the poor nor the rich, but he helped all. To some he gave words of good cheer, being himself stout of heart. Some he encouraged, others he reconciled; to some he gave bodily necessities, to others, clothing. What is wont to happen in all great cities occurred here, too; for on the church porch there was gathered a crowd of people, some unmarried, others married, lying there for their daily food.

3. It happened one time in winter that a woman was lying in labor on the church porch at midnight. He heard her crying out in pain. Leaving his customary prayers, he went out and looked at her. He found no midwife, but instead took the midwife's place, not at all squeamish about the unpleasant aspects of childbirth, for the mercy which worked in him had rendered him insensible to such things.

4. Now his clothes are not worth an obol, and his food is about equally cheap. He can not stand to bend over a writing-tablet—his love of mankind drags him away from books. If someone gives him a book as a present, he sells it immediately, saying to the jeering bystanders: "How can I persuade my Teacher that I have mastered His lessons, unless I sell His own Word[563] to practice perfection?"

69. THE NUN WHO FELL AND REPENTED

1. A certain maiden ascetic who lived with the others had practiced asceticism for nine or ten years. She was enticed by a harper and fell. She became pregnant and bore a child. She came to hate her seducer so intensely and, being moved to the depths of her soul, arrived at such a state of repentance that she straightway tried to kill herself by starvation.

2. Then she prayed and begged God: "Great God, who tolerates the evil of every creature and wishes not the death and loss of those who stumble,[564] if You desire me to be saved, show Your wonders in this present situation and take away the fruit of my sin to which I have given birth, so that I may not hang myself or throw myself overboard." She was heard in her prayers, for the child died not long afterwards.

3. From that day she never again met with the man who had ensnared her, but she gave herself over to the strictest fasting and provided for the sick and the crippled for thirty years. In this way she was so urgent upon God that He revealed to one of the holy priests: "This one has pleased me more in her conversion than in her virginity."

This I write so that we may not condemn those who make a genuine conversion.

70. THE LECTOR CALUMNIATED

1. A maiden, daughter of a priest in Caesarea of Palestine, fell, and she had been coached by her despoiler to accuse a certain lector[565] in the city. And as she was now pregnant and her father was asking questions, she put the blame on the lector. The bishop called the priests together and had the lector called in also.[566] The whole matter was investigated and the lector, upon being questioned, did not confess—for how could he admit something which had never happened?

2. The bishop was vexed and spoke to him severely: "You will not confess, you wretched and miserable man, glutted with impurity?"

The lector replied: "I told you that it was not of my doing. I am innocent of any design upon her. But if you insist on hearing something, even if it is not true, then I did it."

When the lector said this, the bishop deposed him.[567] Then he came to the bishop and said: "Well, since I have made a mistake, command her to be given to me in marriage, for I am no longer a cleric, nor is she a maiden."

3. Then he gave her over to the lector, supposing that the young man would stay by her and could not help but continue his relations with her. But the young man took her from the bishop and her father and entrusted her to a monastery of women. He enjoined the deaconess of the sisterhood[568] there to care for her until it was time for the child to be born.

It was not long before it was the time for her to give birth. The decisive hour had come. Sighs, pangs, labors, visions of the underworld—and still the child was not born!

4. Then passed the first, the second, the third day, a week—the woman, in hell with her pain, did not eat, drink, or sleep, but kept calling out, saying: "Miserable me, I am in danger for having accused this lector falsely."

They hurried off and told this to her father. He was afraid of being condemned as an informer and kept his peace for two more days. The young lady did not die, but she also did not deliver her child. As they could no longer bear her outcries, they ran and told the bishop: "This woman has confessed, crying out for days now that she falsely accused the lector."

Then the bishop sent deacons to the lector with a message for him: "Pray that the woman who accused you falsely may deliver her child."

5. He gave them no answer, he did not even open the door, but he had been praying to God from the day he went inside.

Again the father went to the bishop and prayers were recited in church—and still she did not give birth. Then the bishop got up and went to the lector, knocked on the door, went in, and said to him: "Eustathius, arise, and make loose what you closed."

At once the lector knelt down with the bishop and the woman was delivered of the child. His prayer and persistence had prevailed both to show the chicanery and to teach a lesson to the one who had made the false accusation. From this we may learn to devote ourselves to prayer and to know its power.[569]

71. THE BROTHER WHO IS WITH THE WRITER

1. I shall be finished with my history after I have said a few words about the brother who has been with me from youth until this very day.[570] I know that for a long time he has not eaten from desire nor fasted from desire. I suspect that he has overthrown the lust for riches, which is the biggest part of vainglory. He is satisfied with what he has at hand; he is even thankful if despised, and he does not adorn himself in the matter of dress. He is willing to run risks over and above the line of duty where genuine friends are concerned. He has undergone a thousand or more temptations from demons, as, for example, the day a demon even told him to make a compact with him and said: "Agree to commit sin only once and name any woman alive, I will bring her for you."

2. At another time again the demon buffeted him severely for fourteen nights, so he said, and dragged him by the feet and spoke loudly to him in the night: "Do no more homage to Christ and I shall stay away from you." But he gave his answer: "For this I shall fall down before Him and praise Him a thousand times more since this is so disgusting to you."

He traversed one hundred and six towns, and even stayed in most of them for some time, but by God's grace he has had no traffic with a woman, not even in a dream, except in resistance.

3. I know that at least three times he received necessary food from an angel. One day he was in the innermost part of the desert without a thing to eat. He found three

fresh loaves in his sheepskin. On another occasion it was wine and loaves. Still another time I know someone told him: "You are in want! Go and get grain and olives from this man." So he went to the man to whom he had been sent and asked: "Are you So-and-so?" And the man answered: "I am. Someone has ordered thirty pecks of grain and twelve pints of oil for you."

4. *For such an one I will glory*,[571] whoever he may be. I knew him to weep often on the behalf of men who were lost in poverty, and he gave to such as these everything but his own body. I knew him to mourn over those who had fallen into evil, and in such cases he often brought the fallen one back to conversion. He once certified on oath that he prayed to God that he would goad no one, especially the rich and the sinful, to give him anything for his needs.

5. Now for me it is enough that I was deemed worthy to commemorate all these things which I have now put in writing. For not without God's knowledge was your mind moved to prescribe the composition of this book and to commit to writing the lives of these saints. Now you, most faithful servant of Christ, follow these men gladly, and take their lives and labors and great perseverance as a fitting proof of the resurrection. Follow them willingly, and be nourished by this great hope now that you notice your own days becoming shorter.

6. Pray for me, and keep yourself as I knew you from the consulate of Tatian[572] up to the present day, and as I found you when you were appointed prefect of the most religious bedchamber. For such a one, one whom such

riches and honor and power did not make less God-fearing, reclines upon the Christ who heard the devil say: *All these will I give thee, if falling down thou wilt adore me.*[573]

FINIS

NOTES

LIST OF ABBREVIATIONS

AA.SS.	Acta Sanctorum, ed. by the Bollandists (Antwerp and Brussels 1643–)
AB	Analecta Bollandiana (Brussels 1882–)
ACW	Ancient Christian Writers
Bardenhewer	O. Bardenhewer, *Geschichte der altkirchlichen Literatur*. 5 vols. (Freiburg 1902–32)
Butler	C. Butler, *The Lausiac History of Palladius* (Texts and Studies: Contributions to Biblical and Patristic Literature 6, in 2 vols.: 1 [Cambridge 1898] *Prolegomena;* 2 [Cambridge 1904] *The Greek text edited with introduction and notes*)
Coleman-Norton	*Palladii Dialogus de vita sancti Johannis Chrysostomi*, ed. P. R. Coleman-Norton (Cambridge 1928)
CSEL	Corpus scriptorum ecclesiasticorum latinorum (Vienna 1866–)
DACL	Dictionnaire d'archéologie chrétienne et de la liturgie (Paris 1907–53)
DCB	*Dictionary of Christian Biography, Literature, Sects and Doctrines*, ed. W. Smith and H. Wace. 4 vols. (London 1877–87)
Dialogus	Palladius' *Dialogus de vita sancti Joannis Chrysostomi*
DTC	Dictionnaire de théologie catholique (Paris 1903–50)
Festugière	A. J. Festugière, *Les moines d'orient*. 2 vols. (Paris 1961–62)
JThSt	Journal of Theological Studies (London 1900–05; Oxford 1906–)
Krottenthaler	S. Krottenthaler, *Des Palladius von Helenopolis Leben der heiligen Väter* (Bibliothek der Kirchenväter 5, Munich 1912)
Linnér	S. Linnér, *Syntaktische und lexikalische Stu-*

	dien zur Historia Lausiaca des Palladios (Uppsala 1943)
LTK	Lexikon für Theologie und Kirche. 2nd ed. (Freiburg 1957–)
Lucot	A. Lucot, *Palladius. Histoire Lausiaque* (Paris 1912)
Mackean	W. H. Mackean, *Christian Monasticism in Egypt to the Close of the Fourth Century* (London 1920)
Meursius	I. Meursius, *Palladii Episcopi Helenopoleos Historia Lausiaca* (Lyons 1616)
MG	Patrologia graeca, ed. J. P. Migne (Paris 1844–55)
ML	Patrologia latina, ed. J. P. Migne (Paris 1857–66)
Mus.	Le Muséon. Revue d'études orientales (Louvain 1881–)
ODC	*The Oxford Dictionary of the Christian Church,* ed. F. L. Cross (Oxford 1961)
O'Leary	De Lacy O'Leary, *The Saints of Egypt* (London 1937)
PGL	*Patristic Greek Lexicon,* ed. G. W. H. Lampe et al. (Oxford 1962–)
Quasten *Patr.*	J. Quasten, *Patrology*. 3 vols. thus far (Westminster, Md.-Utrecht-Antwerp): 1 (1950) *The Beginnings of Patristic Literature;* 2 (1953) *The Ante-Nicene Literature after Irenaeus;* 3 (1960) *The Golden Age of Greek Patristic Literature from the Council of Nicaea to the Council of Chalcedon*
RE	A. Pauly-G. Wissowa-W. Kroll, *Realenzyklopädie der klassischen Altertumswissenschaft* (Stuttgart 1894–)
RSR	Recherches de Science Religieuse (Paris 1910–)
SCA	Studies in Christian Antiquity (Washington D.C. 1941–)
Souter	A. Souter, *A Glossary of Later Latin to 600 A.D.* (Oxford 1949)
Tillemont	L. Tillemont, *Mémoires pour servir à l'histoire*

ecclésiastique de six premiers siècles. 16 vols. (Paris 1693–1712)

TLL   Thesaurus linguae latinae (Leipzig 1900–)

TWNT   *Theologisches Wörterbuch zum Neuen Testament,* ed. G. Kittel (Stuttgart 1933–)

VA   St. Athanasius, *Vita Antonii* (MG 26.835–976)

INTRODUCTION

[1] *Hist. Eccl.* 4.21.

[2] The *Life of Saint Antony*, translated by the present writer, appears in ACW 10 (1950) 17–98. Cf. also Quasten *Patr.* 3.20–79 on Athanasius and his works, including (39–45) a treatment of and extensive bibliography on the *Vita Antonii*.

[3] Given in VA 16–43 (= ACW 10.33–57).

[4] Cf. the Prologue to VA (= ACW 10.17): "The rivalry you have entered on with the monks in Egypt is excellent, determined as you are to equal or even to surpass them in your practice of the ascetic life. . . ." Cf. also ACW 10.106, n. 1.

[5] Prologue to VA (= ACW 10.17).

[6] The Greek is λιθομανία and the word is Palladius' own in *Dialogus* 6, termed there by Coleman-Norton a *hapax legomenon*. A similar coinage is found in Isidore of Pelusium, *Ep.* 1.152; Isidore calls Theophilus τὸν λιθομανῆ . . . καὶ χρυσολάτριν. Sozomen (*Hist. Eccl.* 8.12) states that Isidore said it was better to restore the bodies of the sick, which are more properly the temples of God, than to build walls.

[7] The evidence is all gathered in Butler 1.2 f., 173–83, and 2.237–47. A readable account based on this evidence may be found in Coleman-Norton xv-xxvii. Cf. also Bardenhewer 4.148–57; Quasten *Patr.* 3.176–80.

[8] Cf. *Hist. Laus.* 35.8 f.

[9] Cf. *Dialogus* 71. Brisson is mentioned in a list of exiled bishops who had sided with St. John Chrysostom and is addressed in Chrysostom's *Epp.* 190 and 224.

[10] Cf. *Hist. Laus.* 44.1 and 48.2.

[11] Cf. *Hist. Laus.* Prologue 2.

[12] Cf. *Dialogus* 48 ff.

[13] Cf. *Hist. Laus.* 58.1.

[14] Cf. *Hist. Laus.* 45.1.

[15] Cf. Socrates, *Hist. Eccl.* 7.36.

[16] The Greek title is Περὶ τῶν τῆς Ἰνδίας ἐθνῶν καὶ τῶν Βραχμάνων. On the authorship question, cf. P. R. Coleman-Norton, "The Authorship of the Epistola de Indicis Gentibus et de Bragmanibus," *Classical Philology* 21 (1926) 154–60. Coleman-Norton

refutes arguments against Palladian authorship, and he makes the observation (159) that, as in the *Historia Lausiaca* and the *Dialogus*, "sententious observations and proverbs abound" in this work and "an inordinate amount of space is devoted to food and drink . . . or abstinence from them." Cf., however, Quasten *Patr.* 3.180, where it is stated that of the four parts of this work, "only the first seems to be from (Palladius') pen," while the "second and third part are perhaps by the historian Arrian; the fourth by an unknown Christian author."

Quite recently the first attempt in modern times to give us a true Greek text of the account in this work of Indians and Brahmans was made by J. Duncan M. Derrett in "The History of Palladius on the Races of India and the Brahmans," *Classica et mediaevalia: Revue danoise de philologie et d'histoire* 21 (1960) 64–135, which includes (100–135) a critical edition of "Palladius: De vita Bragmanorum narratio, *alias* Palladii de gentibus Indiae et Bragmanibus commonitorii necnon Arriani opusculi versio ornatior." Only the *narratio* proper, the Διήγησις Παλλαδίου εἰς τὸν βίον τῶν Βραγμάνων (loc. cit., 108–113), concerns us here. In a short rhetorical prologue the author says that he had never been to India, but that he had gone as far as the borders of that country in the company of a bishop Moses of Adoule, and that his knowledge of the Brahmans was from a Theban *scholastikos*. The diction and style are Palladian, and the author may well indeed have been our Palladius. Certainly no one has ever conclusively proved that the author of this one piece on India was not our Palladius.

[17] This work, composed about the year 400 and translated into Latin by Rufinus of Aquileia, is similar in content to the work of Palladius. The Latin text may be found in ML 21.387–462; the Greek text was published by E. Preuschen, *Palladius und Rufinus* (Giessen 1897) 1–131. For the various recensions, cf. Butler 1.268–76.

[18] On these *Sayings of the Fathers* (or *Elders*) in various versions, cf. the comments and extensive bibliography in Quasten *Patr.* 3.187–9.

[19] Cf. *Hist. Laus.* 8.6. Cf. also R. Draguet, "Une nouvelle source copte de Pallade: le chap. VIII (de l'Histoire Lausiaque)," *Mus.* 60 (1947) 227–55.

[20] Cf. Quasten *Patr.* 3.177; J. Muyldermans, *Evagriana Syriaca: Textes inédites du British Muséum et de la Vaticane* (Biblio-

thèque du Muséon 31, Louvain 1952) *passim;* R. Draguet, "L'Histoire Lausiaque, une oeuvre écrite dans l'esprit d'Évagre," *Revue d'histoire ecclésiastique* (1946) 321–64.

[21] Cf. H. Weingarten, *Der Ursprung des Mönchtums* (Gotha 1877). This had appeared previously in *Zeitschrift für Kirchengeschichte* 1 (1876) 1–35, 545–74, and the author later answered his critics in his article "Mönchtum" in Herzog-Plitt, *Encyclopädie für protestantische Theologie* 10 (1882) 758 ff.

[22] Cf. O. Zöckler, "Palladius," in Herzog-Plitt, *Encyclopädie für protestantische Theologie* 11 (1883) 173–5; also the same author's *Askese und Mönchtum* (2nd ed. Frankfurt a.M. 1897).

[23] Beginning with his doctoral dissertation, *De Historia Lausiaca quaenam sit hujus ad Monachorum Aegyptiorum historiam utilitas: adjecta sunt quaedam hujus historiae Coptica fragmenta inedita* (Paris 1887), Amélineau dealt in a masterly way with the whole question of early Coptic monasticism in a series of some fifteen books and studies listed in Butler 1.107 f.

[24] For articles attacking the reliability of Palladius, cf. P. Peeters, "Une vie copte de St. Jean de Lycopolis," AB 54 (1936) 359–83; W. Telfer, "The Trustworthiness of Palladius," JThSt 38 (1937) 379–83 (on ch. 35 of the *Lausiac History*); R. Draguet, "Le chapitre de l'Histoire Lausiaque sur les Tabennésiotes dérive-t-il d'une source copte?" *Mus.* 57 (1944) 53–146 and 58 (1945) 15–96 (against the trustworthiness of ch. 32).

[25] Butler 2.iii f.

[26] Cf. Butler 1.77–96.

[27] Cf. E. A. W. Budge, *The Book of Paradise: being the Histories and Sayings of the Monks and Ascetics of the Egyptian Desert. The Syrian texts, according to the recension of Anan-Isho of Beth Abhè, edited with an English translation* (2 vols., London 1904). This was a sumptuous limited edition which included an edition of the Lady Meux manuscript No. 6. Later an inexpensive reprint of the English translation, with notes and introduction, was brought out: *The Paradise or Garden of the Holy Fathers, being Histories of the Anchorites, Recluses, Monks, Coenobites, and Ascetics, Fathers of the Deserts of Egypt between A.D. CCL and A.D. CCCC circiter, compiled by Athanasius, Palladius, Bishop of Helenopolis; St. Jerome and others* (2 vols., London 1907).

[28] Cf. ACW 10.15 and 104 f.

[29] Cf. E. A. W. Budge, *Oriental Wit and Wisdom, or, The*

"*Laughable Stories*," Collected by Mar Gregory John Bar-
Hebraeus (London 1899). Cf. also Butler 1.95 f.

[30] Cf. Butler 1.97-104. This section in Butler on the Armenian
version was contributed by J. Armitage Robinson.

[31] The following (cf. Butler 1.102) will provide an example:
In the *Life of Evagrius* it is told "how he came to the remote
places of Rebon (Arm.: *hreboni*)," which makes pure nonsense.
This "Rebon" appears again in the *Life of Melania*, where, however, the phrase μονήρη βίον occurs in the original Greek. The
Armenian translator may have read this as μονη ρηβιον and then
rendered it to read "the desert of Rebon."

[32] Cf. Butler 1.107-155. Cf. also W. Till, *Koptische Heiligen
und Märtyrerlegenden* (Orientalia Christiana Analecta, Rome
1955), for a fragment of a Coptic life of St. John of Lycopolis.

[33] Cf. Butler 1.155-8.

[34] Cf. Butler 1.159-71.

[35] Cf. O. Hansen, *Berliner sogdische Texte II* (Akademie der
Wissenschaften und Literatur in Mainz, Abhandlungen der
geistes- und sozialwissenschaftlichen Klasse, 1954, Nr. 15); also,
É. Beneveniste, "Études sur quelques textes Sogdiens chrétiens,"
Journal Asiatique 243 (1955) 297-337, esp. 316 ff.

[36] Cf. C. Butler, *The Lausiac History of Palladius* (Texts and
Studies: Contributions to Biblical and Patristic Literature 6, in 2
vols.: 1 [Cambridge 1898] *Prolegomena;* 2 [Cambridge 1904]
The Greek text edited with introduction and notes).

[37] Cf. E. W. Watson, "Palladius and Egyptian Monasticism,"
The Church Quarterly Review 44 (1907) 105-128, esp. 106.

[38] Cf. C. H. Turner, "The Lausiac History of Palladius," JThSt
6 (1905) 321-55; Bonnet in *Revue des études anciennes* (1904)
341-7.

[39] Cf. his articles "Palladiana I: The Lausiac History: Questions
of Text" and "Palladiana II: The Lausiac History: Questions of
History," JThSt 22 (1921) 21-35 and 138-55.

[40] "Palladiana I," JThSt 22 (1921) 35.

[41] Cf. E. Schwartz, "Palladiana," *Zeitschrift für die neutesta-
mentliche Wissenschaft und die Kunde der älteren Kirche* 63
(1938) 161-204, esp. 201 f.

[42] Cf. *Mus.* 63 (1950) 229.

[43] Cf. R. Draguet, "Le chapitre de l'Histoire Lausiaque sur les
Tabennésiotes dérive-t-il d'une source copte?" *Mus.* 57 (1944)
53-146 and 58 (1945) 15-96; and "Une nouvelle source copte de

Pallade: le ch. VIII (Amoun)," *Mus.* 60 (1947) 227–55.

[44] Cf. R. Draguet, "Un nouveau témoin du texte G de l'Histoire Lausiaque (MS. Athenes 281)," *Mélanges Paul Peeters* (= AB 67) (1949) 300–308.

[45] Butler et sa Lausiac History face à un ms. de l'édition I[e] Wake 67," *Mus.* 63 (1950) 203–230.

[46] Cf. D. J. Chitty, "Dom Cuthbert Butler and the Lausiac History," JThSt N.S. 6 (1955) 102–110.

[47] Cf. R. Draguet, "Butleriana: Une mauvaise cause et son malchanceux avocat," *Mus.* 68 (1955) 239–58.

[48] Butler (2.xxiv ff.) gives a very full account of all preceding editions, and yet Butler's own edition must in a very real sense be looked upon as the *editio princeps*, created as it was from a heterogeneous mass of manuscripts, early versions, and printed books. For a just estimate of the man and his work, cf. D. Knowles, *The Historian and Character and Other Essays* (Cambridge 1963) 264–362: "Edward Cuthbert Butler: 1858–1934. I. Abbot Butler: A Memoir; II. The Works and Thought of Abbot Butler" (this is reprinted from the *Downside Review* 52 [1934] 347–465, but without the complete bibliography of Butler given in the earlier version, 466–72).

[49] A. Lucot, *Palladius, Histoire Lausiaque* (*Vies d'ascètes et des pères du désert*). *Texte grec, introduction, et traduction française* (Textes et documents pour l'étude historique de Christianisme 15, Paris 1912).

[50] Dom Antoni Ramon i Arrufat, *Palladi Història Lausíaca: text revisat i traducció* (Fundació Bernat Metge, Escriptors Christians, III Sèrie, 24, Barcelona 1927).

[51] Cf. Ramon, *op. cit.*, xxxiv.

[52] W. K. L. Clarke, *The Lausiac History of Palladius* (Translations of Christian Literature, Series I: Greek Texts, London 1918).

[53] S. Krottenthaler, *Des Palladius von Helenopolis Leben der heiligen Väter* (Bibliothek der Kirchenväter 5, Munich 1912).

[54] *Lavsaik ili zivotopis na svv. otci ot prepodobnij Palladija episkop Elenopolski* (2nd ed. Sofia 1940). This work, which was not available to me, is reported in Linnér.

[55] H. F. Johannsen, *Den Hellige Antonius' Liv og andre Skrifter om munke og helgener i Aegypten Palaestina og Syrien* (Udgivet af Selskabet til Historiske Kildeskrifters oversaettelse 13.4, Copenhagen 1955).

TEXT

FOREWORD

[1] This Foreword is found in only some of the manuscripts of the *Historia Lausiaca* and not in those of the best tradition. Butler (2.xlvii, 3, 182 n. 1) thought that it could safely be rejected as one of the spurious (metaphrastic) additions. Cf. also R. Draguet, "L'inauthenticité du proémium de l'Histoire Lausiaque," *Mus.* 59 (1946) 529–34, and "Un nouveau témoin du texte G de l'Histoire Lausiaque," *Mélanges Paul Peeters* (= AB 67) (1949) 303.

[2] Cf. above, Intro. pp. 3 f.

[3] τελείῳ φρονήματι. Cf. Phil 3.15: ὅσοι οὖν τέλειοι, τοῦτο φρονῶμεν.

[4] On the saints as God's "athletes," cf. H. Delehaye, *Les passions des martyrs et les genres littéraires* (Brussels 1921) 211 f. Terminology of the ancient athletic events was used by St. Paul (Eph. 6.12; 1 Cor. 9.24; Phil. 3.14; 2 Tim. 4.7; etc.) and the early Christian writers to portray the struggle of the Christian to win eternal reward. Cf. below, n. 233; also ACW 10.121, n. 179, and the additional literature there cited.

[5] Cf. the Letter to Lausus following this Foreword; also n. 9 below.

[6] It is true that the *Lausiac History* is not a stylistic gem. It is written in the *koine*, or Common Greek, which was the language of the entire Hellenic world from the end of the third century B.C. to the beginning of the sixth century A.D. The language and the syntax of the *History* are reminiscent on the whole of those of the New Testament Greek. As was noted in the Introduction, the Foreword and the two other introductory pieces, the Letter to Lausus and the Prologue, are written in a more literary—and more stilted—Greek than is the *History* proper.

[7] ἐν τῷ σκάμματι τῆς εὐσεβείας. Σκάμμα, "that which is dug," "trench," then "arena," is often used symbolically, as, for example, in St. Clement of Rome's *Epistle to the Corinthians* 7: "for we are in the same arena (ἐν τῷ αὐτῷ σκάμματι) and face the same conflict" (= ACW 1 [1946] 13). Cf. n. 4 above.

[8] The word "saints" here as well as in other places in Palladius is hardly to be taken as having the full meaning ordinarily given

the word today. The Greek ἅγιοι and the Latin *sancti* were frequently used in early Christian writing for members of the living Church on earth. Cf. H. Delehaye, "Le mot *Sanctus* dans la langue chrétienne," AB 28 (1909) 161-86; also the same author's observation in his brilliant essay, "De martyrologii Romani origine fontibus fide historica" in *Propylaeum ad Acta Sanctorum Decembris* (Brussels 1940) xvii: *in libris antiquis homines sive moribus sive etiam dignitate venerandi sancti appellantur, qui proprie sancti non sunt.* Cf. also H. Joly, *The Psychology of the Saints* (tr. G. Tyrrell, London 1908) 22.

LETTER TO LAUSUS

⁹ This letter, or perhaps a version thereof from which this text stems, was sent by Palladius along with the *History* proper. The addressee, Lausus, was at the time chamberlain at the court of Theodosius II.—On the office of πραιπόσιτος (scil. κουβικουλάριος), cf. J. E. Dunlap, *The Office of the Grand Chamberlain in the Later Roman and Byzantine Empires* (New York 1924).

¹⁰ There are a number of plays upon words in Palladius, and here we have a good example. While others are building material things, constructing them of stone (λίθους οἰκοδομούτων), Lausus desires to be taught the words of true edification (λόγος οἰκοδομῆς). The verb οἰκοδομεῖν means primarily "to build," but also has a derived meaning, "to build character," "to edify." The Latin *aedificare* had the same semantic development; cf. TLL 1.927. On puns in general in the Church Fathers, cf. L. Spitzer, *Linguistics and Literary History* (Princeton 1948) 21, 35 f. Cf. also the present writer's paper, "Proverbs and Puns in Palladius, *Historia Lausiaca*," presented at the Fourth International Conference on Patristic Studies held at Christ Church, Oxford, September 16-21, 1963; this paper is to appear in a forthcoming volume of the *Studia Patristica*.

¹¹ Palladius' angelology is similar to that given in St. John Damascene, *De fide orthodoxa* 2 f., and John Damascene (*De cael. hier.* 8.1) attributes a like opinion to Dionysius the Areop-

agite; but apparently there is no literary connection between the three writers.

[12] Matt. 11.29.

[13] Cf. St. Augustine, *Conf.* 1.1: . . . *fecisti nos ad Te, et inquietum est cor nostrum, donec requiescat in Te.*

PROLOGUE

[14] The introductory part of this Prologue, which is modeled on the Prologue to the Gospel of St. Luke, in the Greek consists of a long periodic sentence running some 39 lines in the text of Butler.

[15] For the Tabennesiotes, cf. below, ch. 32.

[16] Phil. 1.23.

[17] Prov. 24.27.

[18] Cf. Eccli. 7.40: "In all thy works remember thy last end, and thou shalt never sin."

[19] Cf. Prov. 31.8 f.

[20] Eccli. 8.9.

[21] This would have been the Eastern Roman Empire from the standpoint of the Greek writer Palladius.

[22] Gal. 1.18.

[23] A reminiscence of Matt. 18.24.

[24] 1 Tim. 1.9.

[25] Cf. Gen. 43.34.

[26] Pythagoras is said to have prefaced his work *On Nature:* "I swear by the water I drink . . ." (cf. Diogenes Laertius, *Vit. Philosoph.* 8.6), and he elsewhere condemned drinking to excess (cf. *ibid.* 8.9). Diogenes taught his students to be content with plain fare and water to drink (cf. *ibid.* 6.31). Plato (cf. *ibid.* 3.39) advised moderation in the drinking of wine but permitted drinking to excess during the Dionysiac festivals.

[27] Mark 2.18.

[28] Matt. 9.11. This is a question in the Vulgate: "Why doth your Master eat with publicans and sinners?"—There are a number of such variations, some more significant than others, in Pal-

ladius' quoting of Scripture. It is not considered necessary to point out each of these variations in these notes.

[29] Matt. 21.32.

[30] Matt. 11.18 f.

[31] Cf. Gal. 5.6: "For in Christ Jesus neither circumcision availeth any thing nor uncircumcision, but faith that worketh by charity."

[32] Rom 14.23.

[33] Matt. 7.16.

[34] Gal. 5.22.

[35] Gal. 5.22.

[36] 1 Cor. 9.25.

[37] ἀκηδία, defined in PGL 62 as "listlessness, torpor, boredom," which could be bodily or spiritual, the special temptation of monks and hermits. Chaucer speaks of the "synne of accidie," and Aldous Huxley has an essay, "Accidie," in his *Essays New and Old* (New York 1927) 47–53, in which he urged that the word be brought back into English usage. Cf. also below, n. 72 to ch. 5.2.

[38] This passage is difficult in the Greek as well as in English, and the text is probably corrupt. The meaning, however, is clear. Just as one can more easily see and read something written in a very fine hand if one moves closer to a window (to get better light), so one can better direct his life if he does it in the light of the lives of the saints.

[39] Eccli. 19.27 (= LXX Sir. 19.30).

1. ISIDORE

[40] The reference here is to Theodosius I, surnamed the Great, who was emperor from 379 to 395. Cf. DCB 4.959–64.

[41] For this Isidore, cf. also Palladius' *Dialogus, passim*. He is also mentioned in Socrates, *Hist. Eccl.* 6.9; Sozomen, *Hist. Eccl.* 8.2; Theodoret, *Hist. Eccl.* 4.21. Cf. also DCB 3.315; AA.SS. Jan. I (1643) 1015 ff. His feast is celebrated on January 15.

[42] Nitria was a desert area south of Alexandria and about 35 miles west of the westernmost branch of the Nile. It was known to Strabo; cf. his *Geogr.* 18.1.23. Cf. DCB 4.47; RE 17.774 f.— The Greek word here translated "mountain" is ὄρος ; while the

primary meaning of the word is "mountain" or "hill," there was usage of the word for "desert," without apparent regard for elevation.

[43] In pagan times the baths, especially in the larger cities, were great edifices notorious for the immorality associated with them. The early Christians shunned these places as occasions of sin and so preferred physical to moral uncleanness. In *Dialogus* 13, Palladius speaks of the "disreputable baths, hidden from sight, for effeminate men." On the avoidance of baths and even of washing, cf., e.g., in the present volume, chs. 38.12 and 55.2; for other examples and literature, ACW 10.119 f., n. 171.

[44] Heb. 11.32.

[45] According to Porphyry, *Vita Plotini* 1, Plotinus was ashamed even to have a body.

[46] About the year 340 Athanasius, in exile for the second time, made a journey to Rome and Isidore may have been with him at the time. Cf. Socrates, *Hist. Eccl.* 4.23.

[47] Probably this is Bishop Demetrius of Pessinus in Galatia, a faithful friend and supporter of St. John Chrysostom. Cf. DCB 1.804.

[48] VA 3 (= ACW 10.20) tells us that St. Antony also entrusted his sister to a group of holy virgins.

[49] εἰς τὰ λεγόμενα ἐρημικά. Cf. PGL 548.

[50] The word here for "mile" is σημεῖον, "sign," "landmark," "boundary," and used also of milestones. Elsewhere (chs. 18.6; 31.4; 58.4) for "mile" (i.e., the Roman mile of about 5,000 feet) Palladius uses μίλιον, a loanword from the Latin *milium* (rare, but cf. TLL 8.980) or *mille* (scil. *passuum*).

2. DOROTHEUS

[51] Palladius mentions two archimandrites by the name of Dorotheus who lived in his day. Cf. below, ch. 30; also DCB 1.900 f. —Sozomen, *Hist. Eccl.* 6.29, has the same story as given here.— Palladius mentions yet another Dorotheus, a priest, in ch. 58.2 below.

[52] ἀββᾶ, ἀββᾶς, from the Syriac, was a term of reference used for the older monks, and hence became the title used in addressing the superiors of religious communities. Note also the

usage in Mark 14.36. Cf. PGL 2; also W. Jennings, *Lexicon to the Syriac N.T.* (Oxford 1926) 13.

[53] According to the Syriac version, he had made the Sign of the Cross over the water.

3. POTAMIAENA

[54] Cf. ch. 1 above.

[55] However, neither this Isidore nor Potamiaena is mentioned in the VA.

[56] Potamiaena was a celebrated martyr whose feast is on June 28.

[57] Maximian was Roman emperor with Diocletian from 286 to 305, and also held power during part of the turbulent period between then and his death in 310/311.—According to Eusebius, who is probably in error here, the martyrdom of Potamiaena occurred in the year 203 or 204 during the reign of Severus. On the dating, cf. Butler 2.185 f., n. 10.

[58] Eusebius, *Hist. Eccl.* 6.5, gives the judge's name as Aquila. Potamiaena is said to have been sentenced to death and put in charge of a soldier named Basilides, and to have appeared to this Basilides in a vision three days after her death. Basilides became a convert and suffered martyrdom soon afterward.

[59] Swearing by the head of an emperor is mentioned frequently in late Latin literature. Is this present instance, however, possibly a reminiscence of Matt. 5.36: "Neither shalt thou swear by the head . . ."?

4. DIDYMUS

[60] Cf. Matt. 5.4 and Ps. 36.11.

[61] Didymus the Blind, as he is known, was born about 313 and, as Palladius tells us here, lost his sight at the age of four. Despite this handicap, he became a man of great erudition and produced a number of writings, very little of which, however, has survived. He was appointed by St. Athanasius to head the catechetical school at Alexandria, and his pupils included St. Jerome, St. Gregory of Nazianzus, and Rufinus. Jerome, *De vir. ill.* 109, mentions Didymus as a good scholar, the author of commentaries

and a treatise on the Holy Spirit which Jerome himself translated into Latin (ML 39.1031–86). Cf. also Socrates, *Hist. Eccl.* 4.25; Sozomen, *Hist. Eccl.* 3.15; Theodoret, *Hist. Eccl.* 4.26. For an appraisal of the man and his works and modern bibliography, cf. Quasten *Patr.* 3.85–100.

[62] ὁ ἀπὸ ὀμμάτων γενόμενος, where ἀπὸ means "deprived of," "bereft of," as similarly in ἀπὸ ὀμμάτων ὑπῆρχεν in the following. Cf. PGL 189; Linnér 38.

[63] According to Sozomen, *Hist. Eccl.* 3.15, Didymus learned to read with his fingers from raised letters.

[64] Ps. 145.8 (= LXX Ps. 146.8).

[65] The incident here recounted is not mentioned in VA, but is in Socrates, *Hist. Eccl.* 4.25.

[66] Julian the Apostate, who was emperor from late 361 to 363, during his short reign attempted to replace Christianity with paganism. In order to promote dissensions among the Christians, he allowed exiled bishops to return to their sees.

[67] In early 362, shortly after Julian's accession, Athanasius had returned from exile (cf. n. 66 above), but not long later was exiled once more, to return again only after Julian's death in 363.

[68] For further "same day and hour" incidents, cf. VA 60 (= ACW 10.70 ff.); Theodoret, *Hist. Eccl.* 3.19; the Venerable Bede, *Vita Cuthberti* 4.

5. ALEXANDRA

[69] ἐκοιμήθη. "Sleep" for "die," a poetic usage found in earlier pagan authors, was a frequent Christian euphemism. For the fuller concept of "fallen asleep through Jesus," cf. 1 Thess. 4.14: τοὺς κοιμηθέντας διὰ τοῦ Ἰησοῦ. "Sleep" is the usual term with Palladius; note that in ch. 8.5 below, he says that Amoun "died," ἐτελεύτησε, and then immediately adds: "I should say, rather, that he went to sleep" (μᾶλλον δὲ ἐκοιμήθη). For the various expressions meaning "to die" in Palladius, cf. Linnér 124. On death as sleep for the early Christians, cf. also A. C. Rush, *Death and Burial in Christian Antiquity* (SCA 1, 1941) 1–22.

[70] σχηματίσασα. Lucot sees in this word an implication of the word σχῆμα in the meaning of "monastic habit."

[71] Cf. below, chs. 46 and 54. The Melania here is the famous Melania the Elder.

[72] ἀκηδία, recognized as one of the great evils of the solitary life. Cf. St. John Climacus, *Scala Paradisi* 13; Thalassius, *Centuriae* 3, 51; St. John Damascene, *De octo spiritibus nequitiae* 1; and for the remedy, Joannes Moschus, *Pratum spirituale* 142. Cf. also n. 37 above.

6. THE RICH VIRGIN

[73] 1 Cor. 6. 9.

[74] Ps. 23.3 f.–The parenthetical phrase inserted between the question and the answer of the psalm is not at all clear. The Greek is: ἀντὶ τοῦ, σπανίως. Quite possibly the text is corrupt.

[75] I.e., to "bleed" her.

[76] Cassian, *Coll.* 14.4, mentions this Macarius who had charge of the *xenodochium* in Alexandria. There are at least five and possibly six persons with the name of Macarius in the *Historia Lausiaca;* cf. chs. 15.1; 17.1; 18.1; 20.2 f.; 62.–In the following, "coins" = νομίσματα.

[77] On entreating a person by embracing his feet, cf. also VA 60 (= ACW 10.71).

[78] Act 2 of the apocryphal *Acts of Thomas* (tr. M. R. James, *Apocryphal New Testament* [Oxford 1953 corr. rev.] 371–5) tells a similar story of St. Thomas the Apostle, who is said to have received money from an Indian king to build a palace. He spent the money on the poor, thus building this king a palace in heaven. When the king's brother died and wished to live in this palace in heaven, he was told that it was really built by his brother because of contributions the king had unwittingly made to the poor. The king's brother then came back to earth and was converted. R. Reitzenstein, *Hellenistische Wundererzählungen* (Leipzig 1906) 77, believed that this was the source of Palladius' account.

7. THE MONKS OF NITRIA

[79] On Nitria and the more important monks there, cf. the extensive note in Butler 2.187 ff.–The lake named Marea in the first paragraph of this chapter is identical with Lake Mareotis, known also as Mariut or Maryut.

[80] Arsisius was also styled "the Great" by Sozomen (*Hist. Eccl.* 6.30). He was a contemporary of St. Antony but survived him. Cf. DCB 1.174.

[81] Poutoubastes was also mentioned in Sozomen, *Hist. Eccl.* 3.14 and 6.30. Cf. DCB 4.522.

[82] This would appear to be the only mention of Asius as one of the Desert Fathers.

[83] Cronius had been a disciple of St. Antony and served as interpreter for him. Cf. below, ch. 21; also *Vitae patrum* 7.19; DCB 1.716.

[84] This is Sarapion (also spelled Serapion) the Great, another contemporary of St. Antony. He is mentioned in Sozomen, *Hist. Eccl.* 3.13 f., as one who maintained the Nicene doctrine. St. Jerome, *Ep.* 108.14, includes him among the monks visited by Paula in 386. Sarapion the Great is also mentioned by Palladius in ch. 46.2 below.

[85] On the music of the psalmody, cf. St. John Chrysostom, *In Matt.* 8.4 f. The late Cardinal D'Alton included this passage in "Purple and Other Patches" in his *Selections from St. John Chrysostom* (London 1940) 362 f. Athanasius, in his *Epistula ad Marcellinum de interpretatione psalmorum,* in which he praises the Psalter, refers to singing of the psalms and says that this liturgical custom was introduced not for its musical effect but to give worshippers more time to meditate on the meaning.

[86] Cf. VA 60 (= ACW 10.71 ff.).

[87] Pachomius was the founder of the famous monasteries of Tabennisi and he wrote the first monastic rule. Cf. ch. 32 below on Pachomius; also n. 271.

[88] Archimandrite is a term used in the Eastern Church since the fourth century. It was applied originally to the head of a monastery, but now is used for a superior over a group of monasteries. Cf. ODC 79; PGL 240.

8. AMOUN OF NITRIA

[89] Amoun (also Amon, Ammon, originally the name of an Egyptian deity) was another contemporary of St. Antony and filled much the same place in the development of monasticism in Lower Egypt as Antony had done in the Thebaid. His feast is celebrated on October 4. He is mentioned in VA 60 (= ACW

10.71 f.). Cf. also Socrates, *Hist. Eccl.* 4.23; Sozomen, *Hist. Eccl.* 1.14; DCB 1.102; Mackean 81 f.; also R. Draguet, "Une nouvelle source copte de Pallade," *Mus.* 60 (1947) 227–55.

⁹⁰ The crowning of the bridegroom still persists in certain of the Eastern Churches. There is Old Testament authority for this in Cant. 3.11; Isa. 61.10; Ezech. 16.12. However, Tertullian, *De corona* 13, objected to it as a pagan practice.—For an account somewhat similar to that given here of voluntary continence in a forced union, cf. St. Jerome, *Vita Malchi* 6.

⁹¹ According to Socrates, *Hist. Eccl.* 4.23, he read 1 Cor. 7.

⁹² Cf. VA 3 (= ACW 10.20).

⁹³ Cf. above, n. 69.

⁹⁴ According to *Historia monachorum* 30, Amoun's wife joined a community of pious women.

⁹⁵ Cf. above, Intro. pp. 3 f.

⁹⁶ According to Sozomen, *Hist. Eccl.* 1.14, this was a canal branching out from the Nile, possibly at Lycopolis in Upper Egypt.

⁹⁷ For the account of this incident, cf. VA 60 (= ACW 10.71).

9. OR

⁹⁸ Or (also Hor; cf. DCB 3.155) was a contemporary of both Rufinus and Palladius. Sozomen, *Hist. Eccl.* 6.28, places him in the Thebaid, whereas Palladius has him in Nitria. It is possible that he lived on the border and ruled monasteries in both areas. Jerome, *Ep.* 133.3, makes him an Origenist heretic; on Or and his suspected Origenism, cf. Butler 1.177, n. 2.

⁹⁹ Cf. chs. 46 and 54 below on Melania.

10. PAMBO

¹⁰⁰ Pambo is mentioned in Socrates, *Hist. Eccl.* 4.23, and Sozomen, *Hist. Eccl.* 3.14. He stood out among the Egyptian solitaries as a defender of the Nicene doctrine. Some of his *apophthegmata* have survived. He died in 393. His feast is kept on July 18. For other stories about him, cf. AA.SS. July I (1719) 30–35.

¹⁰¹ These four Nitrian monks were called the "Tall Brethren" because of their stature. Palladius treats of Ammonius in ch. 11.

Dioscorus became bishop of Hermopolis; Eusebius and Euthymius were presbyters; but all left their charges for the solitary life, according to Socrates, *Hist. Eccl.* 8.12. Cf. also DCB 1.862; ODC 1320.

[102] Cf. Isa. 40.12.

[103] Cf. Mark 12.42; Luke 21.2.

[104] 2 Thess. 3.8. In VA 3 (= ACW 10.21) it is stated that Antony "did manual labor, for he had heard that *he that is lazy, neither let him eat,*" the reference being to 2 Thess. 3.10. On manual labor and the monastic life, cf. A. T. Geoghegan, *The Attitude towards Labor in Early Christianity and Ancient Culture* (SCA 6, 1945) 163–74; also Mackean 83 f.

[105] Cf. Palladius' account of Pior in ch. 39 below.

11. AMMONIUS

[106] Ammonius (sometimes Ammon), already mentioned above in ch. 10.1, was one of the most distinguished of the monks of Nitria. In ch. 46.3 below, he is called Ammonius Parotes (παρώτης), so designated because he had cut off his ear, as is related in this present account. Cf. Nicephorus, *Hist. Eccl.* 11.37; also Butler 2.191, n. 19; DCB 1.102; Mackean 83, 121, 129, 148.

[107] καθ᾽ ὑπερβολὴν φιλόλογος ἦν, where φιλόλογος, as elsewhere in patristic Greek, means "learned in Scripture." On learning and education among the monks, cf. Festugière. 1.24, n. 2.

[108] This was Timotheus, archbishop of Alexandria in 381–385. Cf. Sozomen, *Hist. Eccl.* 7.9; DCB 1029 f.

[109] Cf. also Socrates, *Hist. Eccl.* 4.23, and Sozomen, *Hist. Eccl.* 6.30, for the cutting off of the ear.

[110] Cf. Lev. 21.17 ff.

[111] For this astronomical number of *stichoi,* "verses" or "lines," Krottenthaler has estimated material some 400 times the length of the *Iliad!*

[112] The reference, of course, is to the great Alexandrine teacher and scholar. Origen was born about the year 185. At the age of eighteen he was appointed head of the catechetical school in Alexandria and held that post for many years. He was a brilliant man and a most prolific writer. Although he allowed the philosophy of Plato to influence his theology to too great an extent and fell into dogmatic errors, there seems little doubt today that

this figure of controversy at least wanted to remain an orthodox and believing Christian. He died at Tyre in 253. For a modern appraisal of the man and his works and extensive bibliography, cf. Quasten *Patr.* 2.37–101.

[113] For Didymus the Blind, cf. above, ch. 4 and n. 61.

[114] Pierius and Stephen are mentioned together also in ch. 55.3 below. We do not know who this Stephen was. Pierius was a priest and catechist at Alexandria who apparently suffered during the persecution of Diocletian and later finished out his days in Rome. St. Jerome, *De vir. ill.* 76, describes Pierius as a man of learning and says that he was called "Origen Junior." Cf. Quasten *Patr.* 2.111 ff.

[115] I.e., Evagrius of Pontus; cf. below, ch. 38.

[116] The passage in brackets here is not in the best manuscripts; cf. the discussion in Butler 2.191 ff.—Palladius also mentioned in *Dialogus* 17 that Ammonius' tomb was a cure for shivering spells. —The Rufinianae were so called because the place belonged to Rufinus, who built a palace and a church on his estate in a suburb of Chalcedon, dedicating the church to Saints Peter and Paul. Cf. Socrates, *Hist. Eccl.* 8.17; RE (2 Ser.) 1.1184 f.; J. Pargoire, "Rufinianes," *Byzantinische Zeitschrift* 8 (1899) 429.

12. BENJAMIN

[117] For Benjamin, cf. also Sozomen, *Hist. Eccl.* 6.29; Nicephorus, *Hist. Eccl.* 11.35; DCB 1.312.

[118] On the use of Holy Chrism, cf. below, ch. 18.11, 22.

[119] Cf. Job 2.7.

[120] Dioscorus was mentioned above in ch. 10.1; cf. also n. 101.

[121] This is a reference to Job 12.13–24.

[122] A story of excessive swelling is also told of Judas Iscariot; cf. Papias, frag. 3 (= ACW 6 [1948] 119).

13. APOLLONIUS

[123] This seems to be the only source for this Apollonius, although two others of that name are known from the literature of this period.

[124] ἄσκησιν γραφικήν . . . . Writing considered as an ascetic exercise is mentioned below, chs. 32.12; 38.10; 45.3.

[125] There is an interesting point here: Apollonius had renounced the world (ἀποταξάμενος) yet carried on a profitable livelihood in his old age among the monks. Apparently these monks did not observe too strict a vow of poverty.

[126] The Syriac has: "The place was a desert and was destitute of things of the world."

14. PAESIUS AND ISAIAS

[127] Nothing more is known of these two beyond what Palladius tells us here.

[128] The Syriac version clarifies a point here: "One man made manifest the works of Abraham by his hospitality, and the other the self-denial of Elijah." This might be taken to symbolize the work of the active and the contemplative religious orders.

[129] Cf. Luke 18.22.

[130] Cf. Luke 9.23; 14.27.

15. MACARIUS THE YOUNGER

[131] Butler (2.193 f.) distinguishes seven by the name of Macarius whose names occur in this and the related documents. Cf. also n. 76 above. The Macarius here has been called "the Homicide" (DCB 3.774) and the story recounted here is told the first time by Palladius. It was told later by Cassiodorus, *Hist. Tripart.* 8.1, and Sozomen, *Hist. Eccl.* 7.29.

[132] Cf. n. 79 above.

[133] Sulpicius Severus, *Dial.* 3.8 (CSEL 1 [1866] 205), tells how St. Martin of Tours blew away a demon which sat on Avitianus' back. This is known as *daemonum exsufflatio*, of frequent occurrence in lives of the saints. Cf. TLL 5^2.18–36.

[134] Cf. Exod. 2.12–15.

16. NATHANIEL

[135] Nathaniel is mentioned in DCB 4.6 f. and O'Leary 208, but in each case it is this story of Palladius which is the source.

[136] Cf. n. 69 above.

[137] In VA 6 (= ACW 10.23) the demon appears in the guise of a "black boy"; however, the word "black" was not uncommonly used by the Romans and Pagans, and in early Christian literature, in a transferred moral sense to designate malice or wickedness. Cf. ACW 10.109, n. 35.

[138] ἀγάπη, "love," a word first used in LXX for "love of God," and in the New Testament for "love of God" or "love of Christ." The term was also applied to a common religious meal, thus often *agape* in the evening while the Eucharist was taken in the morning. It fell out of use by the end of the Patristic Age. Cf. ODC 23; DACL 1.775–848; PGL 7 f.; Butler 2.193, n. 25.

[139] Cf. Luke 13.15; 14.5.

[140] Cf. VA 82 (= ACW 10.88 f.) where the heretic Arians are likened to senseless mules.

17. MACARIUS OF EGYPT

[141] It is difficult to separate the various Macarii. The name occurs often in the Latin, Greek, and Coptic martyrologies. O'Leary (181–6) mentions six in the Coptic alone. Cf. also nn. 76 and 131 above. For the present Macarius of Egypt, also surnamed the Elder or the Great, cf. DCB 3.774; LTK 6.1309 f.; Quasten *Patr.* 3.161–8.

[142] Ps. 5.7.

[143] Although Palladius apparently knew of no literary works by this figure, quite a number of writings have been attributed to Macarius of Egypt. These include fifty *Spiritual Homilies* which have been a source of inspiration for mystics even in modern times. On this Macarius and the question of his authorship, cf. Quasten *Patr.* 3.162–8. Cf. also H. E. White, *New Coptic Texts from the Monastery of St. Macarius* (The Monasteries of the Wadi 'n Natrûn 1, New York 1926).

[144] Scete is in the southern part of the great Nitrian desert, lying west of the mouth of the Nile, some sixty miles south of

Alexandria. Macarius was probably the most famous of its monks. Cf. DACL 15.994–1002; LTK 7.602 s.v. "Nitrische Wüste."

145 Ps. 90.10.

146 Cf. 4 Kings 5.20–27.

147 On frequent Communion, cf. also ch. 27.2 below. Cf. also E. Dublanchy, "Communion Eucharistique (fréquente)," DTC 315–522, esp. 517–21 for the third to fifth centuries.

148 Cf. Sozomen, *Hist. Eccl.* 3.14. This passage refers to the Hieracite heresy which denied the resurrection of the body. Hieracas was one of Origen's pupils; he formed a community of men at Leontopolis who comprised a philosophical sect rather than a monastic community. They refrained from marriage, wine, and meat. Cf. J. Kraus, "Hierakas," LTK 5.321.

149 Palladius assumes orders of demons as of angels. Cf. above, Letter to Lausus 1 and n. 11 thereto.

18. MACARIUS OF ALEXANDRIA

150 On this Macarius of Alexandria, who does not appear to have left any writings, cf. Quasten *Patr.* 3.168 f. A Coptic *vita* of this Macarius was published in *Annales du Musée Guimet* 25 (1894) 235 ff. His feast is celebrated on January 2. Cf. AA.SS. Jan. I (1643) 84 ff.; also DCB 3.774; LTK 6.1310.

151 τὰ κέλλια, so called from the number of cells there; cf. *Historia monachorum* 30. Cellia was a desert spot some 70 stadia from Nitria.

152 Palladius went to Cellia in 390 or 391. Cf. Butler 2.245; Coleman-Norton xvi.

153 Cf. VA 4 (= ACW 10.21) where St. Antony is said to have "made it his endeavor to learn for his own benefit just how each was superior to him in zeal and ascetic practice" and then "devoted all his energies to realizing in himself the virtues of all."

154 The Greek text lacks the "a day," but the Syriac version makes it clear that it was but a pound of bread a day. It should be recalled here that this "pound," λίτρα, was by no means the equal of our 16-ounce pound of today. While it is impossible to be precise about modern equivalents of ancient weights and measures, the "pound" here (as also in chs. 10.2 f. and 17.13 above and in ch. 38.10 below) may be considered as equivalent to about 12 present-day ounces.

155 βουκκελᾶτον, from the Latin *buccellatum*, "soldier's ration of hard bread"; cf. TLL 2.2228; Souter 33. The word is not listed in Linnér. For it and other rare Greek words in the *Historia Lausiaca*, cf. the present writer's paper, "Lexical Problems in Palladius' *Historia Lausiaca*," *Studia Patristica* 1 (Berlin 1957) 44–52.

156 Egypt was long known for its gnats; cf. Herodotus 2.95; Aristotle, *Hist. Animal.* 353ᵃ3, 552ᵇ5.

157 Jannes and Jambres (the form is Mambres in the Latin texts) were magicians of Pharaoh who resisted Moses. Cf. 2 Tim. 3.8 and Exod. 7.11 f., 22.

158 Cf. 2 Tim. 3.8.

159 Hence H. Waddell's "finding the way to Scete by the stars . . ." in her fascinating volume, *The Desert Fathers* (New York 1936) 9.

160 On "athletes of Christ," cf. above, n. 4 to the Foreword.

161 Exod. 13.21.

162 The Syriac version here is somewhat more graphic: "And on another occasion the brethren were digging a well in a certain place what was called Thronon, when a serpent which belonged to the class of deadly serpents bit him. Then Macarius took hold of the serpent with his two hands by its upper and lower lip and, grasping it tightly, tore it in two, from its head to its tail, and said to it: 'Since Christ did not send thee, why didst thou dare to come?' "

163 On the use of holy oil, cf. also chs. 12.1 and 18.22.

164 It is doubtful that the reference here is to the great Pachomius referred to below in ch. 32 (and also n. 271); for the difficulties, cf. Butler 2.196, n. 31.

165 εἰς γῆρας ἤλασας. Butler states that Macarius at this time was between forty and fifty years of age, hardly an old man. Pachomius presumably meant that Macarius was too old to learn the monastic discipline.

166 Cf. n. 52 above.

167 It would appear from this passage that the superior consulted with his community before admitting a novice.

168 But cf. below, ch. 32.8, where the figure of 1300 is given—though, of course, the number of monks doubtless varied at different times.

169 This recalls what St. Athanasius, VA 4 (= ACW 10.21), remarks about Antony's friendly rivalry with other monks.

[170] καλόγηρος, "reverend," "venerable"; cf. PGL 698. In modern Greek καλόγερος means "monk."

[171] St. Antony also addressed his monks as children; cf. VA 82, 91 (= ACW 10.88, 96).

[172] The same story is told in Sozomen, *Hist. Eccl.* 6.29.

[173] Matt. 17.16.

[174] The story of the hyena is somewhat differently told by Sulpicius Severus, *Dial.* 1.15.—There were many Egyptian monks by the name of Paphnutius, seven of them being listed in DCB 4.184–5, and ten in O'Leary 217–21. This one probably is the Paphnutius, identified by O'Leary (220) as a disciple of Macarius, who was a source for Cassian's knowledge of Macarius.

[175] Cf. Luke 18.43.

[176] Some manuscripts insert the name of St. Athanasius into this story. Butler (2.196 f.) has shown how the phrase ἀθανάτῳ Μακαρίῳ, "to the immortal Macarius," became θαυμασίῳ Μακαρίῳ, "to the wonderful Macarius," and finally μακαρίῳ Ἀθανασίῳ, "to the saintly Athanasius." It should be remembered that the ancient manuscripts were often written without spaces between words and with no distinction between capital and small letters.

[177] Cf. Dan. 6.22.

[178] The Greek and Syriac versions both agree in the details here. Was it possibly some special act of self-denial for a monk to refrain from this act? It is also possible that the text here is corrupt; the Old Latin version reads: *non est locutus otiosum sermonem.*

[179] The monks are represented as forming the vanguard of the Church Militant by their prayers and asceticism. Compare the passage in *Historia monachorum* Prol. 10, where the author speaks of the monasteries which surround the cities and support the inhabitants thereof by their prayers.

[180] The Syriac version gives some interesting evidence here about the copying of these Palladian stories. It refers to a large collection of stories about Macarius falsely attributed to Oronamîs (Hieronymus, Jerome), but the translator reassures his readers that they are by Palladius.

19. MOSES THE ETHIOPIAN

[181] This life is not in the Syriac version.

[182] This Moses was a monk and priest in the Scete Desert *ca.* 395. One of the more striking of the Desert Fathers, he was murdered by barbarians when he was seventy-five. Some *apophthegmata* which bear his name have survived. Cf. Sozomen, *Hist. Eccl.* 6.29; Butler 2.197 (where five monks named Moses are noted). His feast is August 28. Cf. AA. SS. Aug. VI (1868) 199–212; E. Hammerschmidt, "Moses der Aethioper," LTK 7.654; O'Leary 206 f.

[183] Some difficulty attaches to this passage. Butler (2.198, n. 34) noted that he was unable to illustrate this curious piece of demonology. Some manuscripts support the reading δαίμονα, which has been followed here, while others eliminate it in one way or another. Lucot thinks of it as a case of metaphor, which is more than likely. Note that Palladius speaks of himself in ch. 71 below as "the brother who is with the writer," and thus here "the demon who had been with him from his youth" could refer to Moses' own evil inclinations. On the other hand, a Syriac version would give us "Clemon," a person, instead of "demon."

[184] ζαβέρνα, apparently used for a bag or sort of wallet. Cf. Souter 453 s.v. *zaberna*, quoting Diocletian, *Edict.* 2.2.7; also PGL 590, which has but this one example. A variant reading, σάκκον, also occurs.

[185] Cf. n. 144 above.

[186] The Syriac version enlarges upon this: "Even as a dog which comes continually to the cook, and if the man gives him nothing, he will not go there again."

[187] Cf. n. 147 above.

20. PAUL

[188] Pherme, which is mentioned in the *Apophthegmata Patrum*, apparently was one of the mountains to the north of the Wadi 'n Natrûn. Cf. Butler 2.198, n. 35.

[189] Apparently this Paul of Pherme must be identified with Paul the Simple, the subject of ch. 22 below. Cf. Butler 2.177.

[190] Cf. Sozomen, *Hist. Eccl.* 6.29. Actually a sort of rosary was in use at this time. Cf. DACL 1.2338 s.v. "Antinoë."

[191] πολιτικός, so called because he was of Alexandria. Cf. Sozomen, *Hist. Eccl.* 3.14.

[192] According to the evidence amassed by Butler (2.198 f.), Saturday and Sunday received the same observance in Egypt at this time. Cf. also Mackean 85 ff.

21. EULOGIUS AND THE CRIPPLE

[193] Cf. above, ch. 7.3 and n. 83.

[194] This must be the "Outer Mountain" where St. Antony spent twenty years in retirement. It is at Pispir on the east bank of the Nile, about fifty miles south of Memphis. Cf. Butler 2.xcviii for a map of monastic Egypt in *ca*. 400 A.D.

[195] This would be the present-day Fustat, not far from Cairo. Cf. RE 2.2699 f.; also Strabo, *Geogr.* 17.807, 812.

[196] I.e., Heracleopolis, one of the oldest of the Egyptian cities, just south of the Fayum. South of Heracleopolis on both sides of the Nile was the "Great Desert" of the Thebaid.

[197] Cf. n. 194 above.

[198] The names of the two monks who buried Antony are not mentioned in VA, but these are the names given by St. Jerome in his *Vita Pauli* 1.

[199] On the numbers who came to Antony for help and advice or to follow him, cf., e.g., VA 15, 49, 55 (= ACW 10.33, 61, 66).

[200] σχολαστικὸς ὑπῆρχεν ἐκ τῶν ἐγκυκλίων παιδευμάτων, "surpassing in erudition because of the round of studies," i.e., the studies preparatory to professional training, liberal studies. For ἐγκύκλιος παιδεία, cf. A. Gwynn, *Roman Education from Cicero to Quintilian* (Oxford, 1926) 85 f., 145 ff., 177 ff., etc.; also H. I. Marrou, *A History of Education in Antiquity* (New York, 1956), ch. 8 and notes, 406 ff. On monks and study, cf. Festugière 1.75–91, "Le Moine et l'Étude."

[201] A possible reminiscence of Luke 10.34?

[202] πλύνειν is used in Aristophanes and the language of Greek comedy in the sense of "to dress down," "to trim down." Cf. also St. Basil, *Leg. lib. gent.* 7.2.

[203] That is, back where Eulogius had found him.

[204] Had Eulogius perhaps been keeping him on the meager fare of the Egyptian ascetics?

[205] This is additional evidence here of the high regard in which St. Antony was held. St. Athanasius said in the Prologue to VA

(= ACW. 10.17): "Really, for monks the life of Antony is an ideal pattern of the ascetical life."

[206] In VA 72 f. (= ACW 10.80) we are told that St. Antony was "without formal schooling" (γράμματα μὴ μαθών; on this phrase, cf. ACW 10.129) but "had a very high degree of practical wisdom." Cassian, *Inst.* 5.33 f., quotes the abbot Theodore as saying that one who has a pure heart and, as a result, a clear mind, has all that is required for an understanding of the mysteries of Holy Scripture.

[207] χρονοτριβήσας ὁ Κρόνιος, a play on words which it is impossible to reproduce in English. Cf. n. 10 above.

[208] There is some evidence offered by Butler (2.200) in a note on this passage that some Eastern Churches commemorated the dead on the thirtieth day. The Copts kept a "month's mind," presumably a thirty-day period.

[209] Antony did not know Greek and used interpreters when speaking with Greeks. Cf. VA 16 (= ACW 10.33); also G. Bardy, *La question des langues dans l'église ancienne* 1 (Paris 1948) 45 f.; Mackean 126. On the problem of language and interpreters in the *Historia Lausiaca*, cf. Festugière 1.23 ff.

[210] αἰγυπτιστί, which here = "in Coptic," the popular language of Egypt. Cf. G. Steindorff, *Lehrbuch der koptischen Grammatik* (Chicago 1951) 1 ff.

[211] For Antony's vision of the passing of souls, cf. also VA 66 (= ACW 10.75 f.).

22. PAUL THE SIMPLE

[212] This would appear to be the Hierax mentioned by Palladius in his *Dialogus* 105.20. Another Hierax is mentioned in *Dialogus* 103.15. The name also occurs in the *Apophthegmata Patrum* (MG 65.231 f.).

[213] This Paul was surnamed the Simple, as we learn from §13 of this chapter. His feast is celebrated on March 7. Cf. AA.SS. Mar. I (1865) 643–7; also DCB 4.277, where a dozen other monks by the name of Paul are enumerated; Sozomen, *Hist. Eccl.* 1.13; Butler 2.201; O'Leary 223; LTK 8.214.

[214] Cf. Sozomen, *Hist. Eccl.* 1.13, and R. Reitzenstein, *op. cit.* 59 ff., where this story is discussed at length.

[215] ἀνατρέχει τὰς ὀκτὼ μονάς. . . . The Greek μονή, as also the

Latin *mansio*, was used for a stopping-place for rest, but could also refer to the distance between such resting places. Cf. Aetheria, *Peregrinatio in Loca Sancta* 20.12 (CSEL 38.67): *hinc usque ad Nisibin mansiones sunt quinque et inde usque ad Hur, quae fuit ciuitas Chaldaeorum, aliae mansiones sunt quinque . . .;* here *mansio* is used in the sense of "a day's journey," and similar usage is found, for example, in Suetonius and Pliny. Cf. E. Löfstedt, *Philologischer Kommentar zur Peregrinatio Aetheriae* (Untersuchungen zur Geschichte der lateinischen Sprache, Uppsala 1911) 76.

[216] According to VA 12 (= ACW 10.30), bread was sometimes kept a whole year.

[217] σκορπίους ποιμᾶναι, possibly influenced by the ποιμανεῖ ἀνέμους in Prov. 9.12 (LXX).

[218] This implies a set period of probation or novitiate among the Desert Fathers. Cassian, *Coll.* 4.7, says that at first they assigned novices to help in the guest house for a year; if the candidate was considered suitable, his old clothes were given to the poor, but if he was not considered suitable, his clothes were returned to him and he left the monastery.

[219] Cf. Dan. 3.

[220] Cf. Prov. 12.17 (LXX).

23. PACHON

[221] The account of Pachon given here has been wrongly attributed to St. Nilus. Cf. Sozomen, *Hist. Eccl.* 6.29; Cassiodorus, *Trip. Hist.* 8.1 (where Pachon is confused with Pachomius); DCB 4.170; Mackean 121, 127.

[222] For Evagrius, cf. ch. 38 below.

[223] Ps. 103.20.

[224] The lives of the Desert Fathers abound in animal stories. Cf. Mackean 136 f. The story of Macarius and the hyena was told above in ch. 18.27 f. St. Jerome, *Vita Pauli* 16, tells how two lions approached St. Antony while he was digging Paul's grave, licked his hands, and dug the grave themselves. Another story of St. Antony and wild animals is given in VA 50 (= ACW 10.63). Cf. also ACW 10.120 f., n. 178.

[225] Sequuntur: καὶ ἐπὶ τοσοῦτον με κεκίνηκεν ὡς νομίσαι με συγγενέσθαι αὐτῇ.

[226] τοῖς γεννητικοῖς μορίοις.

[227] Προστρίψας τοῦ θηρίου τὴν κεφαλὴν τοῖς μορίοις ...

24. STEPHEN

[228] For this Stephen, cf. Sozomen, *Hist. Eccl.* 6.29; DCB 4.741. Cf. also n. 430 below on the possibility that this Stephen and the Stephen mentioned in ch. 47.7 below may be the same person.

[229] Marmarica was along the coast between Egypt and Cyrene.

[230] Mareotis was a part of Libya bordering on Egypt. On the lake of that name, cf. n. 79 above.

[231] On the discernment of grace, cf. P. Resch, *La doctrine ascétique des premiers maîtres égyptiens du quatrième siècle* (Paris 1931).

[232] The Greek has it: κατ᾽ αὐτοὺς τοὺς τόπους τῶν διδύμων καὶ τῆς βαλάνου ἕλκος ποιήσαντα τὸ λεγόμενον φαγέδαινον. The same account is given in Sozomen, *Hist. Eccl.* 6.29.

[233] To the early Christian life was a battle (*certamen*) between vice and virtue. The Christian was the athlete fighting against Satan. Cf. above, n. 4 to the Foreword. The figure is now completed—"to leave the arena," that is, to quit the world (victoriously), to enter the lists of heaven.

25. VALENS

[234] Palladius refers to this Valens in ch. 47.4 below, but otherwise this Valens does not appear to be mentioned anywhere else.

[235] Cf. 1 Cor. 4.6 ff.

[236] This was Macarius of Alexandria; cf. above, ch. 18 and n. 150.

[237] Valens in his pride and arrogance evidently considered himself better than the monk who brought the gift at the behest of the superior.

[238] Butler (2.79) mentions three manuscripts having the reading ἐπλανήθη instead of the impossible ἐνεπαίχθης.

[239] τὰ ἐναντία τοῖς ἐναντίοις ἰάματα. This proverb goes back at least to Hippocrates, *De flat.* 1. Butler (2.201) has collected other examples from the Latin Fathers. Cf. also St. John Damascene, *Hom. in dorm. B. V. Mariae* 2.19 (PG 96.752D). In

the *Apophthegmata Patrum* the holy Syncletice said: "Animal's poison is cured by still stronger antidotes. So fasting and prayer drive sordid temptation from the soul" (tr. O. Chadwick, *Western Asceticism* [London 1958] 55). On proverbs in the *Historia Lausiaca,* cf. the present writer's paper cited above in n. 10.

240 Cf. Gen. 2.9.

241 Cf. Eccle. 7.15 (LXX): "These things also I saw in the days of my vanity: A just man perisheth in his justice. . . ."

26. HERON

242 Cassian, *Coll.* 2.5, mentions a monk by this name but the identity is not certain. Palladius mentions Heron again in ch. 47.4 below.

243 Cf. Matt. 23.9 f.: "And call none your father upon earth; for one is your father, who is in heaven. Neither be ye called masters (teachers); for one is your master (teacher), Christ." Is Palladius accusing Heron of misquoting or merely misusing Scripture? On Matt. 23.9, note that in E. Nestle's critical edition of the New Testament (20th ed., 1950) we find in the critical apparatus: "διδάσκαλον ἐπὶ τῆς γῆς, *Blass ci.*" Does this mean that Blass found evidence in other sources for the teacher-father variant reading? If so, perhaps Palladius himself was quoting the Gospel text here as he knew it.

244 Probably another proverb. Cf. Butler 2.201 f.

245 An Albanius, possibly the same person, is mentioned also in ch. 47.3 below.

246 This is Ps. 118.

247 Another proverb. Cf. Butler 2.201 and the literature there cited; also n. 239 above. The Syriac version here reads: ". . . even as it is said, 'one good is rooted up by another. . . .' "

248 The verb used here, σκέπτομαι, has the meaning of deliberate planning and thus reinforces the earlier statement that he "fell wilfully. . . ."

249 Omisi: κατ' αὐτῆς τῆς βαλάνου.

250 Note the earlier statement that he "found salvation against his will."

251 Is this to be understood as a public confession, similar to a public chapter of faults? Or is Palladius thinking of the public penance which may have been imposed upon Heron?

[252] Cf. above, n. 69.

[253] Cassian, *Coll.* 2.5, is a chapter on the death of Heron.

27. PTOLEMY

[254] Could this possibly be the Ptolemy addressed by Nilus (*Epp.* 1.3 and 3.8–21) on the honor attached to the monastic life? Cf. DCB 4.518.

[255] κλῖμαξ. In this desert country with rocky terrain a good many places might well be called 'The Ladder.' For a metaphorical use of the word in Patristic Greek, cf. PGL 758.

[256] Krottenthaler translates as "grosse Krüge," and his note to ch. 17.11 above ("a Cilician jar of water") says that Cilician means big or large.—The noun form, κιλίκιον, is defined in PGL 753 both as a liquid measure and as coarse cloth. Thus "Cilician" containers may have been so called because of the amount of water they held; or could they possibly have been made of coarse material, which would allow of some evaporation to keep the water cool?

[257] According to ch. 17.9 above, absence from Communion for five weeks was sufficient to draw the punishment of God. Cf. n. 147 above.

[258] Prov. 11.14 (LXX).

28. THE VIRGIN FALLEN FROM GRACE

[259] σακκοφοροῦσαν. Cf. A. Lambert, "Apotactiques," DACL 1.2623.

[260] κατὰ σκηνὴν ἀνθρωπίνην, "on a human stage." Both pagan and Christian writers of late Antiquity used this theatrical metaphor. Cf. E. R. Curtius, *Europäische Literatur und lateinisches Mittelalter* (Berne 1948) 146 ff.

[261] οὐκ ἦν ὁ φύλαξ τῆς σωφροσύνης, possibly referring to her Guardian Angel. Σωφροσύνη has the meaning of "chastity" in Justin Martyr, *Apol.* 14.2; 15.1.—At this point Butler (2.84) adds in a note an exhortation to Lausus which is found in one of the late manuscripts of Palladius.

29. ELIAS

[262] Elias is mentioned in DCB 2.88 f. as an excellent discipli-
narian (*optimus exercitator*) and a special friend of unmarried fe-
males (*amantissimus virginum*).

[263] Athribé, the present Atripe. Shenoute had established a
monastery of nuns near by and Elias may have been their confessor. Cf. J. Leipoldt, *Schenute von Atripe und die Entstehung
des national-aegyptischen Christentums* (Texte und Untersuchungen N.F. 10 [Leipzig 1903] 1).

[264] Cf. H. Hergt, "Die Traumoperation in der christlichen
Asketik," *Bayerische Blätter für das Gymnasial-Schulwesen* 71
(1935) 64–71.

30. DOROTHEUS

[265] Cf. above, ch. 2 and n. 51.—Mackean (124) finds in this
chapter an "amusing picture."

[266] μνηστευόμενος.

31. PIAMOUN

[267] Piamoun is mentioned in DCB 4.396 but nothing has been
added.

[268] Cf. Mitteis-Wilcken, *Grundzüge und Chrestomathie der
Papyruskunde* 1 (Leipzig 1912) 273, on the different categories
of land in Egypt classified as to supply of flood water, whether
high, low, or normal.

32. PACHOMIUS AND THE TABENNESIOTES

[269] On this chapter, cf. R. Draguet, "Le chapitre de l'Histoire
Lausiaque sur les Tabennésiotes dérive-t-il d'une source copte?"
Mus. 57 (1944) 53–146 and 58 (1945) 15–96. Draguet studied
this chapter in great detail and concluded that it was drawn
ultimately from a document in Sahidic Coptic which came to
Palladius in a Greek translation which he found in Nitria.

[270] Tabennisi was a place near Dendera on the right side of the Nile north of Thebes. The mistaken notion that it was an island is due to an error in the manuscript tradition of Sozomen, *Hist. Eccl.* 3.14, where Ταβέννησις is written Ταβέννη νῆσος.

[271] This is the famous Pachomius who started the first great *coenobium* or monastery of the common life at Tabennisi and was later superior of a number of additional such foundations. His housing of the monks together and the rule he gave to Coptic monasticism in the south of Egypt have earned him the title of founder of cenobitism, the form of monasticism which was to spread throughout the world and which has survived to our times. He died in the year 346. Cf. LTK 7.860 f.; DCB 4.170 f.; and esp. Quasten *Patr.* 3.154–9. A number of early biographies of this great abbot have survived. For the Greek lives, cf. F. Halkin, *Sancti Pachomii vitae graecae* (Subsidia hagiographica 19, Brussels 1932). Cf. also the same author's "L'Histoire Lausiaque et les vies grecques de St. Pacôme," AB 48 (1930) 257–301. Butler (2.204–211) refers to chs. 32–34 of the *Historia Lausiaca* as the Pachomian section and he deals at length with it, giving a wealth of information which we cannot reproduce here. Ch. 32 in particular is the source of much reported about the Desert Fathers in Sozomen, *Hist. Eccl.* 3.14 ff. Pachomius was mentioned earlier by Palladius in ch. 7.6 above.

[272] This tablet is not mentioned in the Greek and Coptic lives of Pachomius. Gennadius (*De vir. ill.* 7) states simply that Pachomius composed his rule under angelic inspiration. The Pachomian Rule may be studied most conveniently in P. B. Albers, *S. Pachomii Abbatis Tabennensis Regulae Monasticae* (Florilegium Patristicum 16, Bonn 1923); this work includes (91–125) also the *Doctrina de institutione monachorum* by St. Orsiesius, one of Pachomius' disciples.

[273] The word λεβιτών, which was evidently used for a monastic garment, apparently occurs only in Palladius; cf. PGL 798 s.v. λευιτόν.

[274] This "mystical alphabet" is described also in the Greek *Vitae Pachomii*. St. Jerome mentioned it in his Latin translation of the Rule of Pachomius, and it was also mentioned in still earlier Coptic accounts. Cf. Butler 2.206 F.

[275] This was aimed at the *gyrovagi*, monks who wandered from one religious house to another, always on the move. Cf. *Regula Sancti Benedicti* 1: . . . *quartum vero genus est monachorum*

quod nominatur gyrovagi, qui tota vita sua per diversas provincias ternis aut quaternis diebus per diversorum cellas hospitantur, semper vagi et numquam stabiles. . . . Later Church Councils were to legislate against these *gyrovagi.*

[276] This would seem to imply a regular investiture in the religious habit. Cf. also Marcus Diaconus, *Vita Porph.* 4, where it is said that Porphyry "went to Scete and in a few days was deemed worthy of the honorable habit."

[277] Butler (2.207) mentions the curious fascination this rule held for visitors to the Pachomian monasteries. This rule is also mentioned in *Historia monachorum* 3 and Cassian, *Inst.* 4.17.

[278] This passage is of great liturgical interest. Palladius states here that there were four daily services, and this is confirmed in the other Pachomian texts, both *regulae* and *vitae* of various monks. Cassian, *Inst.* 2.3, conflicts with this in saying that there were only two daily services *per universam Aegyptam et Thebaidem;* Cassian's statement may have been occasioned by St. Antony's instructions to his monks: εὔχεσθαι συνεχῶς ψαλλεῖν τε πρὸ ὕπνου καὶ μεθ' ὕπνον. For a further discussion, cf. Butler 2.207 f.

[279] Cassian, *Inst.* 3.12, also enjoined a psalm before and after meals.

[280] Cf. also the *Regula Sancti Benedicti* 73, intended to be only a "little rule for beginners," *minima inchoationis regula.*

[281] ἐπιγνώμενα, one who had ἐπίγνωσις of the New Testament, "knowledge," amounting to intuition. Cf. Phil. 1.9; Rom. 10.2; Eph. 4.13; Col. 3.10.

[282] The monks having a rule would be happier and safer than they would be if left to their own particular fancies. But the veteran monk advanced in sanctity had not the need of the same counsels.

[283] A figure of 1400 was given in ch. 18.13 above; cf. also n. 168 above. Cassian, *Inst.* 4.1, says that the number was close to 5,000. In St. Jerome's Latin translation of the *Rule of Pachomius* 4 we find 50,000!

[284] This is probably not the Aphthonius mentioned by Theodoret, *Hist. Eccl.* 5, to whom St. John Chrysostom addressed his letters 70 and 93 (MG 52.647, 656).

[285] Panopolis (Akhmîm) on the eastern branch of the Nile. When Palladius visited this monastery he was close by the great monastery of Shenoute (Schenoudi). As Mackean (110) noted,

it is strange that the Greek and Latin chroniclers of Egyptian monastic life appear never to have mentioned Shenoute and we know of this important figure only from fairly recent manuscript discoveries. There are biographies of Shenoute in Coptic, Arabic, and Syriac. Cf. Quasten *Patr.* 3.186 ff.

[286] The Blemmyes were Ethiopic nomads of the Upper Nile country. The earliest literary mention of them is in Theocritus, *Idylls* 7.114, and we are indebted to the *scholia* to this passage for much of our knowledge of them as well as for some information on the pagan worship of Pan (hence the name of Panopolis) in Upper Egypt. Strabo, *Geogr.* 17.786, and Eusebius, *V. Const.* 1.8, also mention them. In his *Dialogus* 20, Palladius says he was "under guard in the neighborhood of the Blemmyes, a tribe of the Ethiopians, at a place called Syene." Cf. also RE 5.566 ff.

[287] The Latin *Regula* mentioned in Butler 2.211 says that no one could stay in the monastery who did not learn by heart at least the Psalter and the New Testament.

33. THE WOMEN'S MONASTERY

[288] There were three convents for women in the Tabennisi area. One at Tabennisi was founded by Pachomius' sister Mary. Another was founded by Theodore. The convent mentioned here was founded by Pachomius himself and he is supposed to have written the rule, according to what Gennadius says in his *De vir. ill.* 7. Cf. Butler 2.211.

[289] Literally, "banished the excommunicated ones (ἀκοινωνήτους) for a period of seven years." Ἀκοινώνητος could mean "excommunicated," "separated from the community," or "denied Communion."

34. THE NUN WHO FEIGNED MADNESS

[290] Thus not without reason has she been called the "Cinderella of Tabennisi" (thus K. E. Kirk, *The Vision of God: The Christian Doctrine of the Summum Bonum* [London 1931] 190).

[291] The phrase "sponge of the monastery" would appear to be a proverb or an adaptation of one, but a search in the proverb

collections has failed to identify such a saying. The Syriac version has: "She became the broom of the whole community."

[292] 1 Cor. 3.18.

[293] Nothing is known of Piteroum beyond what Palladius tells us here, unless Piteroum is a variant form of Pityrion. Cf. Butler 2.212 on the possibility of identification.

[294] Mount Porphyrites is between the Nile and the Red Sea and is mentioned several times in the monastic literature as the abode of hermits. Cf. Cassian, *Inst.* 10.24; *Coll.* 3.5, 7.26, 24.4. Palladius mentions Porphyrites again in ch. 36.1 below and also in his *Dialogus* 17. Cf. RE 22.313 f.

[295] H. Weingarten, *Ursprung des Mönchtums im nachkonstantinischen Zeitalter* (Gotha 1877) 15, suggested that there was a polite euphemism here, that "she was in the kitchen" meant that she was feeble-minded. Note, however, Palladius' explanatory clause after σαλήν, ("touched"; Lucot: "idiote"; Krottenthaler: "närrisch"), a late Greek word which might have been strange to his readers.

[296] ἀμμᾶς or ἀμμᾶ, corresponding to ἀββᾶς, ἀββᾶ, among the monks. Cf. PGL 89; DACL 1.1306 s.v. "ama (amma)."

35. JOHN OF LYCOPOLIS

[297] John of Lycopolis was second only to Antony among the Egyptian monks, according to Tillemont 10.438. He is mentioned by Cassian, *Inst.* 4.23–26 and *Coll.* 1.21, 24.26. Cf. also P. Peeters, "Une vie copte de St. Jean de Lycopolis," AB 54 (1936) 359–83 (this gives a severe critique of Palladius' accuracy and of Butler's defense thereof); S. Morenz, "Ein koptischer Diogenes: Griechischer Novellenstoff in ägyptischer Mönchserzählung," *Zeitschrift f. ägyptische Sprache und Altertumskunde* 77 (1941); I. Hausherr, "Aux origines de la mystique syrienne: Grégoire de Chypre ou Jean de Lycopolis?" *Orientalia Christiana Periodica* 4 (Rome 1938) 497–520.—J. Muyldermans edits this ch. 35 from Cod. Athen. B.N. 1050 in his "À propos d'un text grec attribué à Jean de Lycopolis," RSR 43 (1955) 395–401.

[298] Lycopolis is the present-day Asyut (Siout), a town in Upper Egypt on the western bank of the Nile. Cf. RE 12.2310–13 s.v. "Lykonpolis."

[299] θόλους.

300 On the miracles of John of Lycopolis, cf. St. Augustine, *De cura pro mortuis gerenda ad Paulinum episcopum* 17 (CSEL 41.655); Sozomen, *Hist. Eccl.* 7.22; E. Amélineau, *Monuments pour servir à l'histoire de l'Egypt chrét. aux IVᵉ-VIIᵉ siècles* (Paris 1888) 650–65; also the miracles listed in his *vita* in AA.SS. Mart. III (1865) 689–96. Cf. also Butler 2.212 ff.

301 Theodosius conducted the war against the Goths in 379–382 A.D.—In 387, Maximus, whom Theodosius had earlier been forced to recognize as emperor of the west outside Italy, drove Valentinian II from Italy; Theodosius attacked and captured Maximus, who was put to death in 388.

302 The pagan rhetorician who was set up as puppet emperor by the Frankish count Arbogast in 392. The army commanded by Eugenius and Arbogast was defeated by Theodosius in September 394; both Eugenius and Arbogast were slain.

303 Although Palladius may have known Coptic, he may not have been familiar with the Sahidic dialect of Upper (Southern) Egypt, and hence an interpreter may have been necessary. Cf. Butler 2.213.

304 Butler (1.296) felt that this Alypius probably was Faltonius Probus Alypius, who was *vicarius Africae* in 378 and in 391 prefect of Rome. It is not clear, however, how the chronology of Palladius' life would permit such identification.

305 Luke 5.31.

306 ἀπετάξαντο, that is, they were converted to the religious life. Cf. PGL 216 s.v. ἀποτάσσω.

307 Luke 9.62.

308 There is a play here on the words ἐπίσκοπος, "overseer," "bishop," and ἐπισκοπεῖν, "to examine," "to supervise," "to peer into." We find this also in the *Dialogus* 9 in the sense that "God is the overseer, the true bishop." H. Moore calls attention to this passage of the *Historia Lausica* in his translation of the *Dialogus* (*The Dialogue of Palladius concerning the Life of Chrysostom* [London 1921]) and he translates: "I bishop the kitchens, the tables, and the pots." Note also in the following the play on the word ἀφορίζω, the several meanings of which allow Palladius to "excommunicate" the bad wine. On the puns in Palladius and elsewhere, cf. above, n. 10.

309 According to Marcus Diaconus, *Vita Porph.* 4, the air in Palestine was drier, with a greater difference in temperature between day and night, but not between seasons.

[310] A reminiscence of 2 Cor. 12.2 f.

[311] The reference is, of course, to the illustrious St. John Chrysostom, one of the four great Fathers of the East and the greatest figure of the school of Antioch. The disturbances connected with Chrysostom and Palladius' defense of him are described at great length in *Dialogus* 9 ff. Cf. also Sozomen, *Hist. Eccl.* 8.13 ff. Palladius had lived a long time with Chrysostom and shared in many of his undertakings, and so holds a high place as his biographer. For an appraisal of Chrysostom and his works and extensive bibliography, cf. Quasten *Patr.* 3.424–82.

[312] Palladius also refers to this time in *Dialogus* 20, saying he was "under guard in the neighborhood of the Blemmyes, a tribe of the Ethiopians, at a place called Syene." Cf. also above, §2 of the Prologue. Syene is the modern Aswan (Assuan).

[313] There is a Coptic fragment published by E. Amélineau (*Mémoires publiés par les membres de la mission archéologique française au Caire* 4.2 [1895] 664) which tells of another visit of Poimenia to John of Lycopolis.

[314] This was midway between Memphis and Alexandria. Cf. RE 17.538 ff.

36. POSIDONIUS

[315] Posidonius is mentioned in DCB 4.445 but this is obviously the source. We know no more about him.

[316] Epiphanius of Jerusalem in his *Enarratio Syriae* (MG 120.264) mentions a μοναστήριον τὸ λεγόμενον Ποίμνιον (sic) in the neighborhood of Bethlehem, and this may have been Posidonius' monastery. Tradition had it that the Poimenium was the place where the angels appeared to the shepherds on the night of Christ's birth. Cf. Butler 2.213.

[317] Cf. above, n. 294.

[318] μετὰ δευτέραν γονυκλισίαν ἐξέβαλε τὸ πνεῦμα. Cf. PGL 322 for the genuflections used in exorcism in other examples.

[319] Thus is the great St. Jerome, translator of the Bible and one of the four great doctors of the Western Church, casually introduced by Palladius. Jerome was born at Stridon in or about the year 347. After a classical education in Rome he made a trip to the north; at Treves he copied some commentaries of Hilary of Poitiers and there also seems to have learned something about

the monks in the Egyptian deserts. Later he himself lived for a time as a hermit in Syria in the desert of Chalcis. Around 379 he went to Constantinople and there became acquainted with Gregory of Nazianzus and Gregory of Nyssa. In 382 he returned to Rome, where he served as secretary to Pope Damasus, devoted himself to the study of Scripture, and gave spiritual direction to a number of noble Roman women who had withdrawn from the world. He left Rome in 385, traveled some in Palestine and in Egypt in 385/386, and finally settled at Bethlehem, where he finished out his life. He died in 419 or 420. On St. Jerome, cf. esp. F. Cavallera, *Saint Jérôme: sa vie et son oeuvre* (2 vols., Paris-Louvain 1922); also T. C. Lawler in ACW 33 (1963) Intro. 3–8; W. J. Burghardt, "Jerome, Saint," *Encyclopaedia Britannica* 13 (1962 edition) 2 f.

[320] On the bad feeling between Palladius and Jerome, cf. ch. 41.2 below; also Butler 1.173 f. and 2.213; J. Brochet, *Saint Jérôme et ses ennemis* (Paris 1905); H. Goelzer, *Étude lexicographique et grammaticale de la latinité de Saint Jérôme* (Paris 1884) 38. Jerome accused Palladius of preaching and teaching the "heresy of Origen"; cf. Jerome's *Ep.* 51.9 and *Dial. adv. Pelag.* Prol. 2.

[321] The reference here is to the famous noble Roman widow named Paula who practiced asceticism under Jerome's guidance. After Jerome's departure from Rome in 385, she, too, had left Rome for the East. At Bethlehem, where Jerome supervised a religious community, she headed a convent for women. She died in the year 404 and her third daughter, Eustochium, succeeded her as head of that convent. Jerome addressed many letters to Paula, and his *Ep.* 108, addressed to Eustochium after Paula's death, contains much biographic detail on her.

[322] Nothing further is known of the Oxyperentius and the Peter here mentioned.

[323] It is possible that this is Simeon the Italian monk and friend of Cassian when in Egypt; cf. Cassian, *Inst.* 5.39. It has also been suggested that he may have been the Solitary Simeon. Cf. DCB 4.678.

37. SARAPION

[324] This Sarapion was surnamed Sindonites from his linen clothing. Cf. DCB 4.614. The Greek menology, however, calls him

"the one from Sidon." Sarapion (Serapion) was a common name in the fourth and fifth centuries. Abbé Nau, *Annales de Musée Guimet* 30 (1893) 51, proves that this is the Sarapion who figures with Thais the Penitent. The bodies of Sarapion and Thais lie in the Musée Guimet in Paris.

[325] εὐγράμματος. The word also occurs in Hephaestio, *Astr.* 1.1, with the meaning of "a good writer."

[326] διαφόραι γὰρ εἰσιν φύσεων, οὐκ οὐσίων.

[327] "Greek" is used a number of times by Palladius with the meaning "Gentile," "pagan"; cf. chs. 54.4, 64.1, 65.1. For similar use by Athanasius, cf., e.g., VA 22 (= ACW 10.38).

[328] ἀρραβών. This word was used in classical Greek for "earnest-money," "pledge," but here is used in a Christian sense for "pledge for salvation." Cf. PGL 229.

[329] τριβωνοφόροι, "wearers of the *tribon* (i.e., the philosopher's cloak)," and βιρροφόροι, "wearers of the *birrus* (a kind of Roman cloak)." The Syriac version has here: "the free men and the soldiers."

[330] Apparently they intended to keep the original coin as a relic or souvenir of Sarapion.

[330a] Presumably this means that they thought he was seasick.

[331] Domninus, whose name also occurs as Domnio, is mentioned in the Roman Martyrology for December 28. Cf. *Propylaeum ad acta sanctorum Decembris: Martyrologium Romanum* (Brussels 1940) 605. Paulinus, *Ep.* 3.3, and Jerome, *Ep.* 47.3, both mention Domnio very favorably. Jerome's *Ep.* 50 is addressed to Domnio.

[332] It is just possible that the reference here is to Asella, whose life of seclusion in busy Rome is described by St. Jerome in his *Ep.* 24. Asella is also the addressee of *Ep.* 45 in the collection of Jerome's correspondence. She is mentioned by name in the present volume in ch. 41.4.

[333] Cf. Gal. 6.14.

[334] Cf. Gal. 1.10.

[335] A similar story is told about St. Philip Neri (1515–95) in H. Joly, *Psychologie des saints* (Paris 1920) 63.

[336] According to a Syriac manuscript, *Vita Serapionis*, mentioned by W. Wright, *Catalogue of Syriac Manuscripts in the British Museum* (London 1872) 695, Sarapion died "at the convent of Pachomius in the desert." There is also manuscript tradition for "in the desert" as well as "in Rome" in the present pas-

sage. Cf. Butler 2.116; DCB 4.614.—In the preceding, "perfect self-control" = ἀπάθεια. On Christian ἀπάθεια —perfect self-control, freedom from passion—the ideal of every true monk and ascetic, cf. ACW 10.126 f., n. 227.

38. EVAGRIUS

337 This chapter is a principal source on Evagrius of Pontus, but it was omitted in some manuscripts because of Evagrius' suspected Origenism. It is lacking in the edition of Meursius since it is not in the Paris manuscript; cf. Butler 2.216 f.—Evagrius was born in Pontus in 346, was a disciple of the Macarii (cf. chs. 17 and 18 above), and was a teacher of Palladius. After 382 he lived for a time in the Nitrian Desert and then afterward in the desert of Cellia. He died in 399. His writings provided textbooks for the ascetics of both the East and the West. He has now been cleared of the charges of being in the errors of Origen. Cf. A. and C. Guillaumont, "Évagre le Pontique," *Dictionnaire d'Spiritualité* 4 (Paris 1961) 1731–44. Cf. also Quasten *Patr.* 3.169–76, where much additional literature is cited.

338 Wisd. 4.13. The Vulgate reads: "Being made perfect in a short space, he fulfilled a long time."

339 Ibora was a place in Helenopontus, a town in Cappadocia, not far from St. Basil's monastery. Cf. Sozomen, *Hist. Eccl.* 3.30; also DACL 7.4–9; RE 9.816.

340 A chorbishop (χωρεπίσκοπος, also ἐπίσκοπος τῶν ἀγρῶν) in the early Church was a bishop of a country district in full episcopal orders, but with restricted powers. A chorbishop could confer only minor orders and was under a metropolitan bishop. The term survives only as an honorary title in the Orthodox church today. Cf. DACL 3.1423–53 s.v. "chorévêque."

341 This is, of course, St. Basil the Great, the greatest of the Cappadocian Fathers. Palladius mentions him again in ch. 45.3 below. For Basil and his works, cf. Quasten *Patr.* 3.204–36.

342 St. Basil died on January 1, 379.

343 Both Socrates, *Hist. Eccl.* 4.23, and Sozomen, *Hist. Eccl.* 6.30, mention the ordination by Gregory of Nazianzus, another of the Cappadocian Fathers. For this St. Gregory and his writings, cf. Quasten *Patr.* 3.236–54.—In the foregoing, "most serene" = ἀπαθέστατος.

[344] Nectarius was patriarch of Constantinople in 381–397.–The "great synod" referred to here is the Second Ecumenical Council, Constantinople I, held in 381.

[345] Sozomen, *Hist. Eccl.* 6.30, gives a short résumé of this vision.

[346] Cf. Exod. 7.14.

[347] μετημφιάσθη, i.e., he changed back to his former dress. He had put off the monastic habit for a time and now resumed his former mode of life. Cf. PGL 854 s.v. μεταμφιάζομαι.

[348] The meaning here, as in ch. 18.2 above, presumably is "a pound of bread a day"; cf. above, n. 154.–In the following, as also in ch. 18.2 above, "pint" = ξέστης, formed from the Latin *sextarius*, a measure of approximately one pint, although the Greek word was also used for "cup," "pitcher."

[349] The meaning here may be that he "wrote," served as a scribe or amanuensis, only as much as was necessary to earn his food.

[350] Oxyrhynchus writing was so called because it was "sharp-snouted" (ὀξύς + ῥύγχος); cf. V. Gardthausen, *Griechische Palaeographie* 2 (Leipzig 1913) 113 ff. The word "oxyrhynchus" here has nothing to do with the place of the same name, although that is what both Clarke (136) and C. H. Turner ("The Lausiac History of Palladius," JThSt 6 [1905] 350) apparently believed. Cf. also Festugière 1.24, n. 2.

[351] The *Antirrheticae* is actually a work of eight books, not three, and deals with the eight evil spirits which keep the monk under attack–the demons of gluttony, adultery, avarice, despondency, irritability, weariness of being a monk, sloth, arrogance. Evagrius was not the author of but is the first literary witness to the doctrine of the eight vices, which preceded that of the seven capital sins.

[352] The Arian heresy, named after its founder Arius, denied the divinity of the Son and of the Holy Spirit. For Arius and his writings, cf. Quasten *Patr.* 3.7–13.

[353] That is, a follower of Eunomius of Cyzicus, who became the leader of Neo-Arianism. He died in 394. For Eunomius and his writings, cf. Quasten *Patr.* 3.306–9.

[354] That is, an adherent of the doctrine of Apollinarius of Laodicea. Apollinarius, who apparently died about 390, had fought vigorously against Arianism, but had gone too far–he gave complete divinity to Christ, but mutilated Christ's humanity. For the man and his works, cf. Quasten *Patr.* 3.377–83.

[355] Evagrius is also quoted in Socrates, *Hist. Eccl.* 4.23. A similar story is told of a monk in *Evagrii Pontici capita practica ad Anatolium* 95 (PG 40.1249D).

39. PIOR

[356] Pior was mentioned by Palladius above in ch. 10.8.

[357] But, as we are told in §2, this did not prevent him from letting his sister see him.

[358] Whether or not she herself was able to write, she presumably felt that word from a bishop would carry weight with them. On St. Antony's respect for bishops and priests, cf. VA 67 (= ACW 10.76).

[359] Not to be confused with Moses the Ethiopian whose story is told in ch. 19 above; cf. also n. 182 above.

[360] Cf. Matt. 8.26.

[361] Possibly there is a reference here to Gen. 26.15, 18–22.

[362] Socrates, *Hist. Eccl.* 4.23, also records that Pior made very light of the matter of eating and in fact used to take his food as he walked along.

40. EPHRAEM

[363] Ephraem the Syrian (*ca.* 306–373) was the greatest writer of the Syrian Church. He left a great mass of writings, poetry, sermons, commentaries on Holy Scripture, and more, which were soon translated into Greek, Latin, and Armenian. It is curious that Palladius should mention him at all; it is only later legend that says that Ephraem visited the Egyptian monks. For Ephraem's life and writings, cf. E. Beck, "Ephräem der Syrer," LTK 3.926–9; also Butler 2.218 f.; DCB 2.137–44; Bardenhewer 4.342–73. His feast is kept on January 28 in the Eastern Church; in the West it was celebrated originally on February 1 but was later moved to June 18. Since 1920 Ephraem has been commemorated as a Doctor of the Church.

[364] Cf. E. Meyer, "Edessa," RE 5.1933–1938.

[365] ἡ ἐσχάτη μακαριότης.

[366] A reminiscence of James 5.2.

41. SAINTLY WOMEN

[367] §§2-5 of this chapter are in brackets, and are so enclosed in the Butler text, because they are a reconstruction from various manuscripts.

[368] γυναικῶν ἀνδρείων, i.e., "manly women." Similar usage may be found, for example, in Aristotle, Pol. 1277[b].

[369] Cf. above, n. 321.

[370] Toxotius was the youngest of Paula's five children and her only son. Paula's husband had also been named Toxotius.

[371] Jerome was mentioned earlier in ch. 36.6. Palladius here, as in the earlier case, speaks of him disparagingly. Cf. above, n. 320.

[372] Eustochium (Eustochia) was the third daughter of Paula. She left Rome for the East with her mother and later succeeded Paula as head of a convent at Bethlehem. Cf. above, n. 321. Eustochium was the addressee of Jerome's Ep. 22 (= ACW 33.134-79), one of the most famous of Jerome's letters which amounts to a treatise on the motivations and rules of conduct for a life of virginity.

[373] There is no other mention of this Vallovicus or of his wife Veneria.

[374] Κόμης, transliterated from the Latin comes, was an imperial designation for officials of various ranks.

[375] That is, her wealth. Cf. Matt. 19.24.

[376] For Theodora, cf. DCB 4.903.

[377] Escya in the Syriac version.

[378] For Hosia, cf. DCB 4.1072 s.v. "Usia"; Tillemont 11.280.

[379] Adolia is mentioned in DCB 1.44 as an old friend and correspondent of St. John Chrysostom.

[380] Not mentioned elsewhere.

[381] Twelve persons with the name Candidianus are mentioned in DCB 1.394 f., but none of them appears to be the one mentioned here.

[382] This name is not mentioned in any of the related texts.

[383] We cannot identify this Theoctistus for certain, although DCB 4.899 f. mentions eight persons bearing this name.

[384] For Sabiniana, cf. DCB 4.573. Tillemont (11.263, 519) regarded her as an aunt of St. John Chrysostom, who in his Ep. 13 had addressed her as "my lady Sabiniana the deaconess."

[385] Cf. above, n. 332.

[386] Abita (Avita), along with her husband Apronianus Turcius

and their daughter Eunomia, is mentioned by Paulinus of Nola (*Carmen* 21), who met them in Rome in 406, a year or so after Palladius. Cf. Butler 2.228 f. Abita and Apronianus are mentioned again by Palladius in ch. 54.4 below.

[387] Cf. preceding note.

[388] Cf. n. 386.

42. JULIAN

[389] Julian was an anchorite near Edessa in the middle of the fourth century. Ephraem of Syria wrote his life and he is commemorated on June 9. Cf. AA.SS. June II (1867) 173–6; also Sozomen, *Hist. Eccl.* 3.14; DCB 3.525.

43. ADOLIUS

[390] There is no other mention of this Adolius.

[391] That is, the psalms were sung by two groups alternately. Cf. PGL 160 s.v. ἀντίφωνος.

44. INNOCENT

[392] On the possibility that this might be Pope Innocent I, cf. Butler 2.219 ff.

[393] τὸ σαρκίον, a diminutive form, possibly used here in a pejorative sense.

[394] The tomb of Lazarus at Bethany (Bethania)? Cf. John 11.1–44.

45. PHILOROMUS

[395] Nothing further is known of this Philoromus beyond what Palladius tells us here.

[396] The reference is to Julian the Apostate, who was mentioned above in ch. 4.4; cf. also n. 66 above.

[397] St. Basil the Great was mentioned above in ch. 38.2; cf. also n. 341 above.

[398] Cf. above, n. 104.

[399] St. Mark, according to tradition recorded by Eusebius, *Hist. Eccl.* 2.16.1 and 24.1, was founder of the Church at Alexandria. According to St. Jerome, *De vir. ill.* 8, St. Mark was martyred at Alexandria in 62 or 63 A.D.

46. MELANIA THE ELDER

[400] Melania the Elder (the diminutive form "Melanium" is also known) was also called "thrice blessed" in ch. 5.2 above. This famous, wealthy Roman widow, of Spanish origin, patroness of Rufinus of Aquileia (mentioned in §5 of this chapter), is also the subject of ch. 54 below. She had left Rome for the East, visited in Egypt, and established a community for virgins in Jerusalem on the Mount of Olives. Her subsequent return to Rome for a time is reported by Palladius in ch. 54.

[401] Palladius seems to have slipped here, since Melania was actually a granddaugher of Marcellinus, according to Rufinus, *Apol.* 2.26, and Paulinus, *Ep.* 29.8. They are probably better authorities on this point, although St. Jerome, *Chron.* 289, also makes her a daughter.

[402] Marcellinus had been consul in 341.

[403] Valens ruled from 364 to 378.

[404] Melania's loss of her husband and her departure for the East are described by St. Jerome in his *Ep.* 39.5.

[405] Cf. above, ch. 10 and n. 100.

[406] Cf. above, 7.3–6 and n. 80.

[407] Sarapion the Great, referred to earlier in ch. 7.3; cf. also n. 84 above.

[408] Not to be confused with the Paphnutius who was also called Kephalas, and who is mentioned below in ch. 47.3, 5.

[409] Cf. above, ch. 1 and n. 41.

[410] Cf. above, chs. 10.1 and 12.1 and n. 101.

[411] The *praefectus Aegypti*, "governor of the province of Egypt," was called *praefectus Augustialis*, "Augustial prefect," after the second half of the fourth century A.D.

[412] Epiphanius, *Adv. Haer.* 72.11 (MG. 42.397), quotes a letter addressed to bishops who had been banished to Diocaesarea and among them appear the names Isidore, Pisimius, and Adelphius as here named.

[413] Cf. above, ch. 11 and n. 106.

[414] Melania's servant named Hylas was with Jerome in Syria and died there in or about 375; cf. Jerome, *Ep.* 3.3 (= ACW 33.31 f.).

[415] καρακάλλιον.

[416] Palladius is probably here defending Melania's grand manner with the magistrate. The clause is difficult, but the meaning seems clear: "For with insensate people you have to display your rank and claim your rights."

[417] Rufinus of Aquileia, who was born about 345 in Concordia and whose controversy with St. Jerome in later years contrasted sharply with the close friendship of the two in their early years, had been with Melania (cf. n. 400 above) in Egypt and subsequently rejoined her in Jerusalem, where he founded a community for men. In 397 Rufinus left the East and returned to Italy. He died in 410.—Rufinus' reputation as a writer rests principally on his translations, often paraphrases, of the works of others (e.g., the *Church History* of Eusebius of Caesarea). His *Commentarius in symbolum apostolorum* (= ACW 20) is perhaps his most important original work. On Rufinus and his writings, cf. F. X. Murphy, *Rufinus of Aquileia, His Life and Works* (Washington, D.C. 1945).

[418] The high praise here for Rufinus stands in contrast to the words of criticism Palladius had for Jerome above; cf. chs. 36.6 f. and 41.2 and n. 320.

[419] This heresy claimed that the Holy Spirit was only an angel of the first order.

47. CHRONIUS AND PAPHNUTIUS

[420] It is not impossible that this Chronius and the Cronius mentioned in chs. 7 and 21 above might be the same person. However, the spelling is different and we would seem to have a different individual here.

[421] We do not know the location of Phoinice.

[422] The word here for "step" is βῆμα, which as a unit of measurement equalled approximately 2½ feet.

[423] The word here for "fathom" is ὀργυιά, which as a unit of measurement was equal to about six feet.

[424] Of this James the Halt nothing more is known.

425 Paphnutius was visited by Cassian in 395 and he was then aged ninety. Cassian's treatise *De tribus abrenuntiationibus* (*Coll.* 3.1–22) is from Paphnutius' conferences with his monks. Cf. DCB 4.184 f. Paphnutius is also mentioned in the *Apophthegmata Patrum*.

426 μὴ ἀναγνοὺς γραφάς, referring here not to Holy Scripture but to works of exegesis.

427 Cf. above, ch. 38 and n. 337.

428 Palladius mentioned an Albanius in ch. 26.2 above; this may be the same person.

429 Is this the abbot Chaeremon represented in Cassian's *Collationes* 11 ff. giving conferences on perfection, chastity, and the Providence of God?

430 Is it perhaps possible that this is the Stephen whose story is told in ch. 24 above? If so, then perhaps the "cancer" mentioned in ch. 24.2 may have been a result of the "libertinism" mentioned here.—Meursius (199) identified Palladius' Stephen with the bishop of Antioch of that name mentioned by Theodoret, *Hist. Eccl.* 2.9.10, but that is highly improbable.

431 Nothing is known of the Eucarpius here mentioned. Meursius (199) attempted to identify him with a bishop whom Pope Liberius had mentioned in a letter recorded in Nicephorus, *Hist. Eccl.* 9.8, but this identification is not likely.

432 Cf. above, ch. 26 and n. 242.

433 Cf. above, ch. 25 and n. 234.

434 Cf. above, ch. 27 and n. 254.

435 Cassian, *Coll.* 3.20, gives an account similar to that which follows here.

436 Rom. 12.8.

437 Reading here αὐτοῦ instead of the αὐτῶν printed by Butler from the manuscripts at his disposal. Palladius' Greek is not always grammatical, however, and our author may well have here used the plural in the sense of "such persons."

438 Ps. 49.16.

439 Ps. 118.66.

440 A reminiscence here of Osee 8.7?

441 Gen. 3.1.

442 Cf. Job 6.6: "Or can an unsavory thing be eaten, that is not seasoned with salt? . . ."

443 Job 40.3.

444 2 Cor. 12.7.

[445] John 5.14.

[446] προτιμήσας κόπρον ἐντέρων εὐλογίας πατρικῆς. Cf. Gen. 25.29–34, although Palladius' choice of words here ("filth of intestines," κόπρον ἐντέρων) is unusual.

[447] Rom. 1.28.

[448] Rom. 1.21.

[449] Rom. 1.26.

48. ELPIDIUS

[450] The Bollandists discussed the possibility of identification with Sant' Elpidio in Piceno, whose feast is celebrated September 2; cf. AA.SS. Sept. I [1868] 378). There would seem to be no reason to connect a place in Central Italy with a Cappadocian abbot, but legend has it that his body was brought there and buried and the spot attracted many pilgrims. However, we may well have to do here with another Elpidius. Meursius (200) attempted to identify Palladius' Elpidius with the Elpidius the Deacon mentioned in some of St. Basil's letters (*Epp.* 63, 78, 138, 205, 206).

[451] Procopius, *De bello vandalico* 4.10.22, describes an inscription in the Phoenician language in Africa made by the Canaanite refugees stating: "We are they who fled before the face of Josue the robber, son of Nun. . . ."

[452] In 1 Macc. 16.15 it is told how Simon and his sons went down to Jericho "and the son of Abobus received them deceitfully into a little fortress, that is called Doch, which he had built. . . ." The place named Ducas and Doch are likely the same.

[453] This Timotheus is mentioned as a chorbishop in St. Basil's *Ep.* 24 and is addressed as such in Basil's *Ep.* 291 as one "who led an upright and ascetic life since boyhood. . . ." Cf. also DCB 4.1128 f.

[454] That is, like a "queen bee," which the Greeks regarded as masculine. Arrian, *Epict.* 3.22.99, used the feminine, "the queen of the bees," but that form was censured by Phrynichus, *Ecloga* 202.

[455] There is nothing else known of this Aenesius.

[456] This Eustathius has also not been identified.

49. SISINNIUS

[457] This Sisinnius has not been further identified, although there were a number of people with that name.
[458] Adapted from Gal. 3.28.
[459] Cf. Tit. 1.8 and 1 Tim. 6.17 f.

50. GADDANES

[460] Sozomen, *Hist. Eccl.* 6.34, mentions a Gaddanes who lived with Azizus and Aones; the source there was in all probability a Syriac original.

51. ELIAS

[461] Elias is mentioned as a solitary of Antinoë in Sozomen, *Hist. Eccl.* 6.29, and this story is told at greater length in *Historia monachorum* 12. Cf. also DCB 2.89.

52. SABAS

[462] Nothing else is known of this Sabas.
[463] κοσμικός, "of the world," here used to differentiate Sabas from those in the religious life.
[464] μόδιος, a "peck-measure," according to W. F. Arndt and F. W. Gingrich, *A Greek-English Lexicon of the New Testament and Other Early Christian Literature* (Chicago 1957) 527. Certainly the "bushel" proposed by Clarke in his translation seems too great a quantity here, where the context would suggest a measure smaller than even a peck.

53. ABRAMIUS

[465] There is no other mention of this Abramius in the literature.

54. MORE ABOUT MELANIA THE ELDER

[466] Cf. above, n. 400.

[467] We do not follow Palladius here. Does he mean that Persia benefited by her gifts? But Persia is not named as receiving gifts. Or does he mean that some special type of Persian (Asiatic) oratory and rhetoric could do more justice to her gifts? Where the text here has "Persia," the Meursius text reads: "Persia, the Britains, and all the islands," but Meursius adds nothing in his notes. Cf. Butler 2.225, n. 92.

[468] The initial letters of the Greek words for east, west, north, and south (ἀνατολή, δύσις, ἄρκτος, μεσημβρία) in the order here given spell "Adam." For literary treatment of this acrostic, cf. F. Dornseiff, Das Alphabet in Mystik und Magie (Στοιχεῖα: Studien zur Geschichte des antiken Weltbildes und der griechischen Wissenschaft 7, Berlin 1925) 137 f.

[469] Her son, Publicola, was referred to in ch. 46.1 above and is mentioned by name in §6 of this chapter. There are some who say that Melania had three sons in all; however, they may be confusing the children of the two Melanias. Note the reference in ch. 61.2 below to the two sons of Melania the Younger.

[470] σπιθαμήν, the space one can embrace between the thumb and little finger.

[471] This is a reminiscence of Rom. 8.35.

[472] Cf. Butler 2.226, n. 94, for the chronology.

[473] Apronianus and his wife Abita were also mentioned in ch. 41.5 above.

[474] Palladius devotes ch. 61 below to Melania the Younger and Pinianus; cf. also nn. 525 and 526 below.

[475] Albina is mentioned further in ch. 61.6 below.

[476] The verb used here is θηριομαχεῖν, "to fight with wild beasts," as in, for example, 1 Cor. 15.32 and St. Ignatius of Antioch, Ad Rom. 5.1, and here with the special meaning "to fight against evil counsels."

[477] 1 John 2.18.—Palladius here has: παιδία, γέγραπται πρὸ τετρακοσίων ἐτῶν ὅτι ἐσχάτη ὥρα ἐστίν. Compare the passage in Dialogus 20: παιδία, ἐσχάτη ὥρα ἐστίν . . . εἰ δὲ πρὸ τετρακοσίων ἐτῶν εἴρηται παρὰ τοῦ ἀποστόλου ἐσχάτη . . . , "Little children, it is the last hour . . . and if the apostle spoke of the last hour four hundred years ago. . . ." This is taken by Butler as a proof of the Palladian

authorship of both the *Dialogus* and the *Historia Lausiaca*—it is "one of those mannerisms or tricks that betray personality and point to unity of authorship" (C. Butler, "Palladiana II," JThSt 22 [1921] 142).

[478] Publicola (died 406) was the son of Melania the Elder; he and his wife Albina were the parents of Melania the Younger. For Publicola, cf. also DCB 4.518 f.

[479] Palladius is here referring, of course, to the sack of Rome by Alaric in 410 A.D.

[480] The destruction of Rome had been foretold in the Sibylline Oracles; cf. *Orac. Sib.* 8.165.

[481] Compare this with the *Vita Melaniae junioris* 19: εὐθέως Ἀλάριχος ἐπέστη τοῖς κτήμασιν οἷς ἀπέδοντο οἱ μακάριοι. Καὶ πάντες τὸν τῶν ὅλων δεσπότην ἐδόξαζον λέγοντες. Μακάριοι οἱ φθάσαντες ἑαυτῶν ἀποδόσθαι, τὰ πράγματα πρὸ τῆς τῶν βαρβάρων ἐπιστασίας.

55. SILVANIA

[482] This chapter is actually a continuation of ch. 54, since it deals further with Melania the Elder rather than with Silvania. The Syriac version combines chs. 54 and 55 in a single, long chapter, and that very likely was the original arrangement.

[483] That is, from Jerusalem. Jerusalem had been renamed Aelia Capitolina by Hadrian in 136 A.D. after the Jewish rebellion had been quelled by the Roman army.

[484] Silvania was a sister-in-law of Rufinus, the minister of Theodosius the Great. Cf. also DCB 4.669; Butler 2.229.

[485] Jovinus, as Palladius tells us here, was a deacon at this time and later was bishop of Ascalon in Palestine. He was appointed bishop before or in 415, as he was present at the Synod of Diospolis that year. Cf. DCB 3.466.

[486] Ascalon (or Ashkelon) was on the Mediterranean coast of Palestine between Gaza and Jamnia. The city was destroyed in 1270.

[487] Pelusium was on the then easternmost branch of the Nile and about 20 miles east of the modern Port Said. It was mentioned by Strabo as surrounded by swamps.

[488] νιπτῆρα λαβόντα νίψασθαι τὰς χεῖρας καὶ τοὺς πόδας πυγμῇ ὕδατι ψυχρωτάτῳ. The language here is reminiscent of that in Mark 7.3: πυγμῇ νίψονται τὰς χεῖρας. It is interesting to compare

the present passage, together with Melania's remarks in the following paragraph, with the passage in *Dialogus* 11 where we are told of the journey of St. John Chrysostom and the welcome refreshment of a bath once his party reached a city or village where such a luxury was available.

[489] The Greek text here has ἐκείνη, "that person," "she." I have supplied the name to prevent ambiguity, as did also Lucot and Ramon in their translations. Krottenthaler, presumably misled by the chapter heading, inserted the name of Silvania.

[490] φιλήσασα τὸν λόγον, in the sense of "loving the Scriptures and the writings of the Church Fathers"; cf. above, n. 107. On Melania the Elder and learning, cf. Festugière 1.77 ff.

[491] Pierius and Stephen were also mentioned together in ch. 11.4; cf. above, n. 114.

[492] 1 Tim. 6.20.

56. OLYMPIAS

[493] Olympias, born about 368, in 384 married Nebridius, a nephew of Emperor Theodosius. Left a widow soon afterwards, she refused to remarry, although Theodosius wished her to do so. Her name occurs in the Roman Martyrology for December 17. Cf. DCB 4.73 ff.; LTK 7.717; also n. 498 below. Palladius gives a short account of her life in *Dialogus* 17, saying that she visited the baths but seldom, only when the state of her health required this, and then she would not enter the water ungarmented, since her modesty forbade her to regard herself.

[494] Nothing more is known of this Seleucus.

[495] ἀπὸ κομήτων. On this special use of ἀπὸ with the genitive to describe one deprived of office, a former official, as also with Ablavius and Nebridius in this same paragraph, cf. Linnér 35 ff. and PGL 189 s.v. ἀπό.

[496] Ablavius had been praetorian prefect and was martyred in 337.

[497] Cf. above, n. 493. Nebridius is mentioned also by Palladius in *Dialogus* 10.

[498] According to Sozomen, *Hist. Eccl.* 8.9, Nectarius, patriarch of Constantinople, made her a deaconess, although she was but a young widow. Later the Council of Chalcedon set the minimum age at forty. On the role of such widows in the early

church and an account of their ministry, cf. J. Viteau, "L'institution des diacres et des veuves," *Revue d'histoire ecclésiastique* 22 (1926) 513–37; also ACW 13 (1951) 121 f., n. 66, where additional literature is cited.

57. CANDIDA AND GELASIA

[499] There is no other mention of this Candida.

[500] The Trajan here mentioned was a commander-in-chief under the emperor Valens. It is possible that this was the person to whom St. Basil had addressed two letters (*Epp.* 148 and 149) in 373. Cf. DCB 4.1042.

[501] Cf. VA 67 (= ACW 10.76), where St. Athanasius remarks that St. Antony "was not ashamed to bow his head before bishops and priests."

[502] Cf. Heb. 12.16; Gen. 25.25–34.

[503] For Gelasia, cf. DCB 2.617.

[504] Cf. Eph. 4.26.

58. THE MONKS OF ANTINOE

[505] Antinoë was a city on the eastern bank of the Nile near the Thebaid. Cf. Butler 2.230; RE 1.2442 s.v. "Antinoupolis."

[506] Solomon (also Salomon) was a solitary who dwelt near Antinoë.

[507] Nothing is known of this Dorotheus beyond what is told here. Two other persons of the same name were the subjects of chs. 2 and 30 above.

[508] Cf. ch. 61.

[509] Also not otherwise known.

[510] Cf. above, n. 200.

[511] Not otherwise known.

[512] ἀπὸ λῃστῶν. On this use of ἀπό, cf. n. 495 above.

[513] Prov. 9.12 (LXX).

[514] κενοδοξία. The fifth *Collatio* of Cassian purports to be instructions from Sarapion on the eight capital sins (cf. above, n. 351) and *cenodoxia* is listed in *Coll.* 5.12. It is stated there, however, that there may be merits in *cenodoxia*, inasmuch as a

man in high position may consider certain sins beneath his dignity.

59. AMMA TALIS AND TAOR

[515] Talis is not mentioned anywhere else. On the title "amma," cf. n. 296 above.

[516] Nothing is known of Taor beyond what Palladius tells us here.

[517] On weekly Sunday Communion, cf. also ch. 32.3 above. Cf. also n. 147 above.

60. THE VIRGIN AND COLLUTHUS THE MARTYR

[518] Colluthus (also Acolluthus), the patron saint of Antinoë, had been martyred in the Thebaid years earlier during the reign of Maximian. His feast is May 20 in the Coptic Synaxary, May 19 in the Greek Menology.

[519] This recalls the passage in *Dialogus* 11 where Basiliscus, who also had been a martyr, appeared to St. John Chrysostom the night before Chrysostom's death and said: "Be of good cheer, brother; tomorrow we shall be together."

[520] That is, Clement of Alexandria, who was born about 150 and died shortly before 215. Clement of Alexandria was often called simply "the Stromatist," the title deriving from the title of his greatest work that has come down to us, his *Stromata.* Cf., e.g., Cassiodorus, *Inst.* 8.4: *Clemens Alexandrinus presbyter, qui et Stromatheus vocatur.* . . . For an appraisal of Clement and his writings, cf. Quasten *Patr.* 2.5–36.

[521] This "composition" on the prophet Amos has not survived. Palladius apparently is the only source that mentions this work by Clement; it is not mentioned in the literary catalogues of St. Jerome and Gennadius. It is perhaps possible that the reference here is to a part of Clement's *Hypotyposeis* (also lost except for some fragments) in which, according to Eusebius, *Hist. Eccl.* 6.14.1, Clement gave "concise explanations of all the Canonical Scriptures. . . ."

[522] This was, of course, none other than Palladius himself.

[523] Cf. ch. 5.1 above, where Alexandra is said to have died "after she had arranged herself"; also *Dialogus* 11, where St. John Chrysostom is reported to have arranged himself for burial in white clothes.

61. MELANIA THE YOUNGER

[524] Cf. above, ch. 58.2.

[525] Melania the Younger was actually the granddaughter of Melania the Elder; cf. n. 478 above. Ancient lives of Melania the Younger have been published by the Bollandists; cf., for the Latin, AB 8 (1889) 16–63; for the Greek, AB 22 (1903) 5–50. Cf. also the late Cardinal Rampolla's *Santa Melania Giuniore, Senatrice Romana* (Documenti contemporanei et note, Rome 1905), a work which has been partly translated into English by E. Leahy and edited by H. Thurston, *The Life of St. Melania* (London 1908).

[526] Pinianus was mentioned by Palladius in ch. 54.4 above. He, with the two Melanias and Albina, was among the well-to-do Catholics who left Rome and went into exile in North Africa at the time of Alaric. St. Augustine's *Ep.* 124 was addressed to Pinianus, Albina, and Melania when they were staying at Tagaste. When Pinianus came to Hippo to meet Augustine, the people of Hippo tried to get him to accept ordination as their priest; this scene is described in St. Augustine's *Epp.* 125 and 126.

[527] Pinianus is mentioned in St. Augustine's *Ep.* 124 as a son of Valerius P. Severus.

[528] 1 Cor. 7.16.

[529] For a description of the sharing of the property, cf. the passages quoted from the *Vita Melaniae junioris* in Butler 2.232 ff.

[530] Nothing further is known of this Paul.

[531] 2 Tim. 4.17.

[532] Referring, of course, to the Visigothic king who had earlier terrorized the inhabitants of Rome and had sacked their city in 410, himself dying later that year. A number of Catholic nobles who left Rome at the time of Alaric took their riches with them.

[533] Albina, the wife of Melania the Elder's son Publicola, was mentioned by Palladius in ch. 54.4 above. Cf. also n. 526 above.

[534] "Eunuchs" here probably is to be taken figuratively, re-

ferring to persons who had "made themselves eunuchs," that is, made firm resolutions to lead single and chaste lives. Cf. Matt. 19.12.

[535] Cassiodorus, *De inst. divin. litt.* 1.28.5–7, enlarges upon the benefits to be obtained from a happy combination of gardening and study.

[536] This was in the year 405 when Palladius went to Rome to plead the cause of St. John Chrysostom. Palladius frequently does not put his facts in chronological order!

[537] That is, John Chrysostom.

62. PAMMACHIUS

[538] Pammachius was a Roman senator of the Furian family which was prominent in the church at Rome in the fourth and fifth centuries. He was a fellow student of St. Jerome in Rome. Jerome later addressed a number of letters to him (*Epp.* 48, 49, 57, 66, 97) and spoke highly of him. Paulinus of Nola also addressed a letter (*Ep.* 13) to him in which he mentions Pammachius' care of the poor. Pammachius died in 409, during the Gothic invasion. Cf. DCB 4.178; LTK 8.16.

[539] Perhaps the Macarius (Macharius) who was a good friend of Rufinus. On the possible identification, cf. DCB 3.775 s.v. "Macarius exvicarius."

[540] ἀπὸ βικαρίας. Βικαρία is a loanword from the Latin *vicaria*. This is the only occurrence of the Greek form cited in PGL 297.

[541] There is no other mention of this Constantius.

63. ATHANASIUS AND THE YOUNG MAIDEN

[542] The great St. Athanasius was forced to leave his diocese of Alexandria a total of five times, and two of these five exiles were during the reign of Constantius II. He had been exiled by Constantine to Treves; Constantine died in 337 and Athanasius returned to his diocese late that year. The opponents of Athanasius continued to work against him, and at the instigation of Eusebius, bishop of Nicomedia, they again deposed him in a synod at Antioch in 339. Athanasius took refuge in Rome; al-

though a synod held there in 341 completely exonerated him, he did not get back to Alexandria until the fall of 346. After the death of Constans in the West in 350 left Constantius sole emperor of East and West, Constantius had a synod summoned at Arles in 353 and at Milan in 355 to condemn Athanasius, who was forced once again to leave—and this apparently is the time of which Palladius is here speaking. Cf. the following note. Athanasius was also exiled once under Julian the Apostate and once again under Valens; but he was finally restored to his post for good in 366, and he spent his remaining days, until his death in 373, in peace. On Athanasius, the man and his works, cf. Quasten *Patr.* 3.20–79.

[543] Constantius II died in 361 and was succeeded by Julian the Apostate. The period of six years Palladius mentions here is that from February 356, the date of Athanasius' expulsion from Alexandria, to February 362, the date of his return. It was during this period of exile, when he fled to the monks of the Egyptian desert, that he wrote his *Apologia ad Constantium imperatorem, Apologia pro fuga sua, Historia Arianorum ad monachos,* and *Epistula encyclica ad episcopos Aegypti et Libyae.*

[544] The date of his return to Alexandria was February 22, 362.

[545] The verb used here is μνηστεύειν, meaning primarily "to court," "to woo," but also used in the sense of "to sue," "to canvass" for something. Note also the usage of this verb in ch. 30 above, "exhorting."

64. JULIANA

[546] Juliana is mentioned also in Eusebius, *Hist. Eccl.* 6.17; cf. also DCB 3.468.

[547] τῶν Ἑλλήνων. Cf. above, n. 327.

[548] Jewish translator of the Hebrew Scriptures into Greek. His translation dates from about 200 A.D.

[549] Cf. Eusebius, *Hist. Eccl.* 6.17, for an almost identical account of this. Eusebius and Palladius must have copied the inscription independently of each other. Cf. also H. B. Swete, *Introduction to the O.T. in Greek* (Cambridge 1902) 49 ff., for a discussion of this passage.

65. HIPPOLYTUS

[550] Is this a reference to Hippolytus of Rome? If so, then "a man who knew the apostles," γνώριμος τῶν ἀποστόλων, can hardly be taken as referring to a person who knew the apostles personally, but rather as referring to one who was closer to and knew better the apostolic period, one who was almost early enough to know the apostles themselves.

[551] The story told here is also told in Nicephorus Callistus, *Hist. Eccl.* 7.13, though it is questionable whether Nicephorus' source was Palladius. Cf. Butler 2.234, n. 114.

[552] Literally, "Greek"; but cf. above, n. 327.

[553] Ὁ δὲ εἰσπραττόμενος τὸν χρυσὸν ἔκδοτον αὐτὴν παρεῖχε τοῖς βουλομένοις.

[554] Ἕλκος ἔχω τι εἰς κεκρύμμενον τόπον ὅπερ ἐσχάτως ὄζει, καὶ δέδοικα μὴ εἰς μῖσός μου ἔλθητε· ἔκδοτε οὖν μοι ὀλίγας ἡμέρας, καὶ ἐξουσίαν ἔχετε καὶ δωρεάν με ἔχειν.

[555] Apparently it was the custom for men to cover themselves when leaving the *lupanar* (cf. Petronius, *Satyricon* 7), presumably to avoid detection by acquaintances.

[556] κατασφραγισαμένη. Κατασφραγίζειν, "to seal," is here used in the Christian sense of "to seal with the Sign of the Cross." Cf. PGL 722.

[557] According to the account in Nicephorus, *Hist. Eccl.* 7.13, he was beheaded.

66. VERUS THE EX-COUNT

[558] This is the present Ankara in Turkey.

[559] There is no other mention of this person for the period of Palladius' life.

[560] Cf. above, n. 495.

[561] This is the only mention of Bosporia.

67. MAGNA

[562] Nilus of Sinai (also Nilus of Ancyra) addressed a treatise, *De voluntaria paupertate* (MG 79.968–1060), to a deaconess,

Magna of Ancyra. This is most probably the person here mentioned.

68. THE COMPASSIONATE MONK

[563] That is, sell a copy of the Gospels.—In one of the manuscripts of Palladius there follows here a story of Bessarion, who sold a little book of the Gospels to provide clothing for a poor man; cf. ML 73.1197D f., *Vita abbatis Bisarionis*. There is also a similar story attributed to Evagrius in the *Apophthegmata Patrum* wherein one of the brethren is said to have had no possessions but a Gospel, sold it to feed the poor, and said: "I have even sold the word which commands me to sell all and give to the poor."

69. THE NUN WHO FELL AND REPENTED

[564] Cf. Ezech. 33.11.

70. THE LECTOR CALUMNIATED

[565] This cleric, an ἀναγνώστης, is addressed in §5 of this chapter as Eustathius.
[566] It is to be noted that in this case the bishop acted as judge in the matter.
[567] According to the *Apostolic Canons* 95, a cleric guilty of fornication was to be deposed.
[568] διάκονον τῆς ἀδελφότητος. For "deaconess," ἡ διάκονος was used as well as the feminine form, διακόνισσα.
[569] This Eustathius was believed later to have suffered martyrdom; cf. DCB 2.391.

71. THE BROTHER WHO IS WITH THE WRITER

[570] Palladius here is referring to himself, employing a literary device to add some autobiographical details. He may have been prompted by the example of St. Paul in 2 Cor. 12.2 ff.: "I know

a man in Christ. . . ." According to Dom Ramon, MS 112 Holy
Sepulchre reads: Περὶ τοῦ βιοῦ ἑαυτοῦ διηγεῖτει ὁ συγγραφεύς.

571 2 Cor. 12.5.

572 This was in 391.

573 Matt. 4.9.

INDEXES

1. OLD AND NEW TESTAMENT

2. AUTHORS

Aetheria
   Peregrinatio in Loca Sancta
   20.12: 187
Albers, P. B., 192
Anan-Isho, 9 f.
Amélineau, É., 8, 164, 196 f.
Aristophanes, 185
Aristotle
   Hist. Animal. 353ª3, 552ᵇ5:
   182; *Pol.* 1277ᵇ: 203
Arndt, W. F., 209
Arrian, *Epict.* 3.22.99: 208
Athanasius, St., 9, 32, 37, 43,
   144 f., 171 f., 182 f., 185, 199,
   213, 216 f.
   Ep. ad Marcellinum de in-
   terpret. ps., 175;
   Vita Antonii, 3, 4, 9, 162
Augustine, St.
   Conf. 1.1: 169; *De cura*
   pro mortuis gerenda ad Pauli-
   num Episcopum 17: 196; *Ep.*
   124: 215

Bar-Hebraeus
   Laughable Stories, 10, 165
Bardenhewer, O., 159, 162, 202
Bardy, G., 186
Basil, St., 111, 122, 137, 196
   Epp. 24, 78, 138, 205, 206:
   208; 148 f.: 213; *Leg. lib.*
   gent. 7.2: 185
Beck, E., 202

Bede, the Venerable, St.
   Vita Cuthberti 4: 173
Beneveniste, É., 165
Blass, F. W., 189
Bonnet, M., 165
Brochet, J., 198
Budge, E. A. W., 164
Burghardt, W. J., 198
Butler, C., 9 f., 12–15, 159, 162,
   164 ff., 176–9, 181–6, 188 ff.,
   192–6, 198, 200, 204, 210, 218

Cassian, 183, 198, 207
   Coll. 1.21, 24.26: 195; 2.5:
   189 f.; 3.5, 7.26, 24.4: 195;
   3.20: 207; 4.7: 187; 5.12: 213;
   11 ff.: 207; 14.4: 174; *De tri-*
   bus abrenuntiationibus (*Coll.*
   3.1–22): 207; *Inst.* 2.3, 4.1,
   4.17: 193; 4.23–26: 195; 5.39:
   198; 10.24: 195
Cassiodorus
   De inst. divin. litt. 1.28.5–
   7: 216; 8.4: 214; *Hist. Tri-*
   part. 8.1: 179, 187
Cavallera, F., 198
Chadwick, O., 189
Chaucer, G., 170
Chitty, D. J., 14, 166
Clarke, W. K. L., 15, 166, 201,
   209
Clement of Alexandria, 141, 214
   Hypotyposeis, 214

3. GREEK WORDS

230

4. GENERAL INDEX

abandonment, 128 ff.; by God, 82, 126; of Esau, 130
abbot, 208
Abita, 119, 135, 203 f., 210
Ablavius, 137, 212
Abobus, 208
Abraham, 25, 50; symbol of hospitality, 179
Abramius, 133, 209
abstention, from spitting, 66, 183; from swearing, 44
abstinence, 27, 138; from marriage, wine, meat, 181
accidents, occur with God's consent, 126
accidie, 170
acrostic, spelling Adam, 210
act, 126; good, 86, 127; evil, 25; of impiety, 109, of indecency, 110
Acta Sanctorum, 170, 176, 181, 184, 186, 196, 204, 208
actors, Greek, 105
actress, 87, 105
Acts of Thomas, 174
Adam, 210
Adelphius, 205
Adolia, 118, 203
Adolius, 119 f., 204
Adoule, 7; Moses of, 163
Adversary, 127
adultery, 201
aedificare, 168
Aelia, 136; Aelia Capitolina, 211

Aenesius, 131, 208
affection, natural, 148
Africa, 143, 208
agape, offerings for, 53
ailments, 28, 102, 136
Akhmîm, 193
Alaric, 143, 211, 215
Albanius, 86, 125, 189, 207
Albina, 135, 143, 210 f., 215
Alexandra, 173, 215
Alexandria, 5, 6, 10, 31, 36, 39, 42, 44, 49, 54, 74, 76, 87, 94, 102 f., 108, 123, 126, 144 f., 170, 177, 181, 184 f., 197, 214, 216 f.; catechetical school at, 172, 177 f.; Church of, 35, 205; monasteries of, 75; *xenodochium* at, 174; martyrdom of St. Mark at, 205; shrine of St. Mark, 123; prefect of, 34; Alexandria a source of temptation, 103
Alexandrian, 62, 86
alms, 127; almsgiving, 25
alpha, 93
alphabet, Greek, 93; mystical, 192
Alypius, 100, 196
amanuensis, 201
Amatas, 72
amma, 214
Amma Talis, 140, 214
Ammon (Ammonius), 177
Ammon (Amoun), 175

233